Patricia A. McLagan

THE SHADOW SIDE OF POWER

LESSONS FOR LEADERS

Changing World Press
Washington, DC
www.changingworldpress.com

For a free *Reader's Guide* and other support to help you implement the lessons and insights in this book, go to:

www.shadowsideofpower.com

REVIEWER COMMENTS

"Ignorance, Myopia, Reductionism, Abdication, Cowardice, Abuse of rank, Corruption, can be faced and overcome when leaders see their work as a calling and inspire meaning making in others. Leaders who make the choice to lead through responsible leadership will help make organizations both safe for their employees and profitable for their investors. What a wonderful allegory. Adderley's journey through leadership shadows should help every leader avoid these pitfalls. Patricia is a creative and insightful writer.
Dave Ulrich, Professor, School of Business, University of Michigan and Partner, The RBL Group

"The Shadow Side of Power is just plain great storytelling—the kind that draws you in, stirs your passions, sustains your interest, teaches meaningful lessons, and leaves you both gratified and wanting more. That's all the more significant when the topic is the dark side of leadership. With skillful writing, imaginative storytelling, and a powerful narrative Pat McLagan takes us on a journey to visit those places that lurk in the shadows. To the places where such sins as ignorance, shortsightedness, narrow-mindedness, cowardice, abuse, and corruption reside. They've never been more entertaining, nor more meaningful and practical, than in this book. Before you embark on your next leadership adventure, take a guided tour through the allegorical world of The

Leadership Inferno. You'll be better prepared for your other challenges once you have."

Jim Kouzes, coauthor of the bestselling *The Leadership Challenge,* and Executive Fellow of Leadership, Leavey School of Leadership, Santa Clara University

"I love it! It is deep, thought-provoking, and spellbinding. I have also never read a management book quite like it. It's unique, challenging, and easy to identify with, and it challenges us in moral ways I have also never read before. An important contribution!!! Although [the book] is for management, it really is for us all. It's all of our paths [and] whether we choose the final path Adderley walks of positions of power or our own unique paths, each of us is confronted by what I see as the ethical issues of relating."

Dr. Stephen Schuitevoerder, Past President and faculty member, Process Work Institute.

"I've read lots of management books and this one is much deeper than most in its approach to power and leadership. It has a good flow to it with the fictional storytelling to illustrate the points. Therefore, enjoyable to read."

Dr. Pat Cataldo, Managing Director – Executive Development at University of North Carolina

"What excites me about Pat McLagan's Inferno is how it tackles both the squandering of power as well as its abuse. Until leaders look hard at these pitfalls, they risk blindly plunging into them. This is one of the most daring and creative treatments on power of our generation. McLagan has given us an unforgettable read. It will be

viscerally absorbed into the internal maps of those who would lead and follow through the flames and heat necessary for serious accomplishment."

Ira Chaleff, Author, *The Courageous Follower*. Former Executive Director, Congressional Management Foundation

"*I truly LOVE the concept presented in* The Shadow Side of Power. *It is a seminal approach to discussing leadership and how its dark side is so alarmingly easy to fall into. McLagan has done a remarkable job of creating a modern day allegory that hits the core of the unfortunately all too true and scary abuses of power we learn about every day in our world. The lessons here are legion and will stick with readers for years after they've digested it, as long as they are willing to face the reality that we all have a little of Adderley's dark side in us. A must read for current and aspiring leadership practitioners, before it's too late.*"

Dr. Steve Cohen, Founder and Principal, Strategic Leadership Collaborative, Inc.

"*This is like a scary movie at times, —with horrible creatures. As I sit on my side porch here in candlelight, I may need to go inside and turn on a bright light!*"

Deborah Santagata, Business Advisor and former Senior Manager, AVAYA

"*I am blown away by McLagan's ability to weave language so artfully and richly! I love the "principles" and "sins" that the book is based on. Relevant, timely, appropriate for all types of leaders across many types of institutions as you demonstrate in characters we meet along the journey! I grinned at the whole-brain example in particular and the disconnected cables with the four colors—well done!"*

Ann Herrmann-Nehdi, CEO, Herrmann International, Inc.

"About halfway through his journey, the main character, Adderley, says to his mentor, 'Peneth, there is too much to absorb here'. Clearly, this feeling of being overwhelmed is a challenge experienced by many thoughtful people who try to do their best in a leadership role. What I appreciate about Pat McLagan's book is that she helps us to handle this challenge. Through evocative storytelling she helps us to find personal meaning in essential leadership lessons."

Donna B. McNamara, Former Vice President, Global Education and Training, Colgate Palmolive Company

This book is dedicated to all leaders who use their formal power for the best interests of the people, institutions, and communities they lead, represent, and serve . . .

and

. . . to my grandchildren, Colin, Kathryn, and Ryan. May you inherit and help create a future where power is increasingly a creative, not a corrupting force.

CONTENTS

Cover
Title Page
Reviewer Comments — III

Prologue — i
Preface — iii
The Calling
    Chapter 1: Adderley at Work — 3
    Chapter 2: The Promotion — 7
    Chapter 3: The Party — 9
    Chapter 4: At Home — 13
    Chapter 5: The Dream — 15
The Gateway
    Chapter 6: The Surrender — 21
    Chapter 7: The Place of No Decision — 25
The Inferno
    Chapter 8: First Circle: The Ignorant — 31
    Chapter 9: Second Circle: The Myopic — 37
    Chapter 10: Third Circle: The Reductionists — 43
    Chapter 11: Fourth Circle: The Abdicators — 51
    Chapter 12: Fifth Circle: The Cowards — 61
    Chapter 13: Sixth Circle: The Abusers of Rank — 69
    Chapter 14: Seventh Circle: The Corrupt
            and Corrupters — 89
The Return
    Chapter 15: Accepting the Calling — 107

Afterword: Leadership as a Mythic Journey — 113
Postscript: A Brief Summary of Dante's Inferno — 115

Footnotes   123
Acknowledgements   127
About the Author   129
Other Books by Patricia McLagan   133

PROLOGUE

My name is Adderley. Before I took on an executive leadership role in the Jada Division of BlythCo International, I had a remarkable and life-changing experience. I became a time traveler in the Leadership Inferno—a place where I faced the dark side of power and where I was almost destroyed by my and others' disowned shadow side.

Whether my experience was "real" or not, I can't say. But, then, what is reality? Every day I oscillate continually between my inner world of thoughts, perceptions, conclusions, and judgments and an outer world where others' perceptions often differ greatly from my own. What I learned from my journey through the Leadership Inferno is that as a person with institutional power, I have unique responsibilities that have broad ripple effects. For, as a formal leader, Jada's and my influence circle are often the same. When I'm in the leader role, I must be an accountable steward of something bigger than me. And, although having formal power is extremely difficult and sometimes fraught with temptations, I now find great satisfaction in taking the challenge and responding to the call to lead.

Today I think and am told that I am a good leader. I'll be the first to admit that I'm not without faults. Rather than deny my shadow sides and the allures of power, I am aware of and learn from them. I draw insights and even strength from recognizing the more selfish choices I could make. Because of my travel through the Leadership Inferno, I am increasingly conscious about my impact and not afraid to step into my formal leadership role. Nor am I afraid to share leadership with others. But that gets ahead of the story.

The truth is that before my meeting with Peneth Tipton and my trip through the Leadership Inferno, I was headed in a different direction. I wish I had met her earlier in my management career, for I would have done many things differently as I moved up the ranks. But teachers do seem to appear when the student is ready. At least that was true for me.

PREFACE

You are about to enter a fantasy world. It is a world where people with formal authority (whether called leaders or managers) who have misused, abused, or simply not used their power for larger good are punished for their omissions and actions. It is also a world that leaders everywhere must understand so that they can transcend it, for there is tremendous energy for personal growth in power's shadow.

My intent in this book is to raise the awareness of people who have *formal* institutional power in all sectors and at all levels: government leaders, business and non-profit executives, supervisors, team leaders, deans, legislators, school principals, anyone whose job it is to make institutional decisions and to align resources–including people–to a larger purpose. My hope is that by facing the temptations that accompany formal power (the "shadow side of leadership"), leaders who read and think about this book will become more conscious of their choices and the impacts of their decisions and actions. I also hope that formal leaders and those aspiring to leadership roles will see the incredible opportunity that accompanies such roles, for aware leadership can result in profound personal growth, wisdom, and impact.

A key assumption in *The Shadow Side of Power* is that formal power evokes the emotional as well as the rational and thus can shape one's view of the world. Leadership and management theories and practices that do not account for this potentially distorting effect of power are destined to remain disconnected from real life and thus remain in the realm of ideas, not action. Worse, formal leaders may use more rational leadership theories and practices to expand their influence for personal gain rather than to advance the best interests of the institutions and stakeholders they serve.

While I have had the privilege of working with many conscientious leaders at all levels in public and private institutions globally, I have long been concerned about the intentional and unintentional, small and large misuses and abuses of power. But this is a difficult topic to write about in a way that has impact beyond the impressions we get from the all-to-frequent newspaper stories about failures of people in power or the complaints of people being led. It is also difficult to write about what appears to be a negative topic without depressing you, the reader, or me, the author.

However, when the global financial crisis hit in 2007 I realized that something had to be done to raise the consciousness of people in formal leadership/management roles everywhere. A key point for all formal leaders to realize is that with disproportionate power comes disproportionate responsibility. Formal leadership is a vocation and a choice. Only those who are vigilant about the temptations of power and committed to the larger good should take on its mantle.

I did not want to write another rational or "how-to" book about leadership/management. There are many of these on the market and, while much of the guidance is educational and worth attention, it generally ignores the very important and distorting emotional factors that come with institutional power. Rather, I wanted to alert formal leaders to the temptations that accompany formal power – to raise consciousness and the awareness of what Jung called the "shadow" in all of us.

There is much in literature that exposes us to the dark side of human nature. Most schools of psychology encourage us to explore our shadows, understand them, and thus be more aware when they tap us on the shoulder. One of the most enduring stories of the human shadow is Dante Alighieri's allegory, "Divine Comedy." Dante lived in 13th century Italy, a time fraught with political and religious intrigue that inspired him to create a fictional journey through hell ("Inferno"), purgatory ("Purgatorio"), and heaven ("Paradiso"). At the time he wrote "Divine Comedy," he was apparently going through a transition in his life. He made himself the central character, the journeyer. In his epic he moves through each of the three worlds with the help of a guide.

For Dante's journey through the nine circles of his Inferno, his guide and protector is Virgil, the author of the famous 1st Century BCE classic poem "The Aeneid."[i] As he moves through the Inferno and the other worlds, it is clear that Dante is on a journey of personal introspection and discovery. He faces his and others' shadow side. He emerges wiser and more self-aware than if he had blocked his shadow and remained in a state of psychological innocence or naïveté. His journey into the shadows is actually a path to the light!

It is my hope that by accompanying our hero, Adderley, on his journey through the seven circles of my Leadership Inferno, everyone reading this book will emerge more self-aware and more conscious of the temptations that inevitably accompany power. There are two major responses to these temptations. One option is to avoid the responsibilities of formal power or, more seriously, to engage in major and minor misuses or abuses of power. A second option is to face into temptation, making active and aware choices to use power for personal growth and positive interpersonal and institutional impact. It is a choice that can only be fully made when we are aware of both the light and the shadows that accompany formal power.

The Shadow Side of Power: Lessons for Leaders is for people who have formal power, but it also helps those without institutional power to appreciate the challenges and demons that come along with any kind of power. It is about the shadow side of management/formal leadership but there are implications for all of us, regardless of formal roles, for we all at some level collude in creating the leadership around us. We often project our own early experiences with authority (with parents, teachers, and others) on those leading us today. By looking into rather than ignoring the dark side of power, we will more easily recognize it, understand where it comes from, transform it, and defuse its destructive effects in ourselves and in others.

This is a short book that invites deep exploration and thought—something very difficult to make time for these days. I use allegory and story as a means of slowing down your thought process and focusing your reflection on the deeper issues associated with the use of formal power. There are many books out there that list concepts, models, and actions for leaders to take. It is easy to scan or rush through them. However, when you are inside a myth—a story—you must slow down and try to decipher the deeper meanings. The rewards for slowing down and reflecting include personal introspection and life impact.

So, prepare for a journey into the Leadership Inferno, the place where sins of omission and commission by those with institutional power are displayed and punished. And be open to using your deeper awareness of the shadow to help you convert the dark side energies that circle around powerful people into potent forces for institutional and personal development and good.

Pat McLagan

Washington, DC

2013

The Calling

CHAPTER 1
Adderley at Work

On the day my life changed, the suburban head office of my company, Jada Corporation, a Division of BlythCo International, was bathed in the light of high summer. Nestled in an environmental park that is known for its green technologies, the designer building felt like a haven even though still under construction.

At the time, I managed a large research group that was developing a breakthrough approach for filtering indoor air. We faced a very challenging deadline and I felt frustrated about the pace of some of the experiments of one of my teams. Looking back, I'm sorry to say that I didn't handle the situation very well.

I rolled up my sleeves and took over the work of our senior researcher. "Here, let me do this checking," I told her, realizing now that I completely negated her accountability and disempowered her. (That's how I did things back then!)

She challenged me. "But, Adderley, we need more time to complete these important tests. I told you this two weeks ago. Didn't you get us an extension?"

I was upset, felt time pressured, and didn't answer directly. "Let's just get this done—I'll patch it," I told her as she walked away. I made a mental note to ask the Human Resources specialist to have a disciplinary talk with her.

Let me put this all in a bit of perspective so you understand what was going on at Jada and its parent corporation, BlythCo International. BlythCo is a conglomerate of mostly traditional companies. It is listed on the stock exchange and has the usual pressures for quarterly performance. Several years ago the company acquired Jada—an outlier for BlythCo, for Jada lives on the leading (some would say "bleeding") edge of green technology. We were told over and over again that Jada was a real risk for BlythCo.

The BlythCo executives reminded us frequently that they had invested tens of millions in us and had yet to turn a profit. They said they were committed, that supporting Jada was the right thing to do for many reasons. They also pointed to our Jada building as a real scion of new green concepts. They said that the products we were making here had great promise. But uncertainties abounded and it still wasn't clear how we would make our division work given the political pressures and quagmires that make change so difficult in our key markets.

We didn't know how long the BlythCo board would go along with the investment in us at Jada.

There were other complications. Pressure for short-term results was also strong because senior executive options were coming due in the next fiscal year. So they were not inclined to make further investments for the future that would take away from the bottom line and deflate share prices.

I knew that we needed to take a different tack, for I understood our market and its immense possibilities. But I didn't have the guts to fight the battle with people above me, even though I had the kind of technical credibility that would have at least raised some eyebrows. I might have been able to buy my group some time even in the situation I just described. Instead of speaking up, I rode the tide, swallowed my frustrations, and looked for a few ways to cut more costs in order for my bottom line to look good for the short term.

Looking back, I am not proud of my behavior, even though I won't demonize the short-term concerns that dominated my actions—for they were important, too. What I did then is all part of the larger ongoing story, and I have come to embrace it as part of my journey to become a better leader and more developed person. Of course, the kind of behavior I engaged in on that summer day was part of the reason I found myself in the Leadership Inferno.

CHAPTER 2
The Promotion

It came as a complete surprise! My boss, Selene, who rarely came to my office, sauntered in and closed the door.

"Adderley, we've made the decision to fill that Research and Development Vice President position. We want you to take that job and do everything you can to make it work for us. Congratulations! You and people like you are the future of our company. Your R&D unit consistently delivers, and we think you will be able to make that happen for the entire department. You can start your new role on the first of next month, and we'll announce it tomorrow. What do you say?"

Well, I must admit that I was shocked, but I felt myself immediately sit taller even as I blurted out the first thing that came to me. "That's really great news. I'm sure I can whip the department into shape and I have lots of ideas that I can implement right away. I really appreciate the opportunity. Thank you!"

Selene shook my hand and left my office. I sat back in my chair, breathless and a bit lightheaded, my thoughts oscillating between the research project I had just taken over and the shift in role that I had just apparently accepted. I felt the pressure increase in the atmosphere around me. My chair creaked as I leaned back, feeling the weight of it all.

CHAPTER 3
The Party

What happened next is a bit of a blur. The following day an announcement about my promotion crawled through our intranet and seeped into the business sections of many newspapers. I had little time to think as people stopped by my office with congratulations and requests. Someone organized an impromptu party at the pub on the outskirts of our office park.

I tried to focus on finishing up the rework of the research I'd intervened in the day before while also thinking about what to bring to my new, more spacious office. Then a bunch of colleagues descended on my office, grabbed the baseball cap I usually wore when I left work, threw it on my head and scuttled me off to the pub.

It was quite a scene. There were a few executives from the corporate BlythCo offices, plus my new vice president peers from Jada and people from the R&D Department that I would soon head.

I spent most of my pub time talking with my new executive peers, glancing from time to time at clusters of people from lower organization levels. They seemed to be gossiping quietly and I caught a slight note of concern— but this was only fringe awareness. The overall tone was celebration, and I was happy with that.

Jada people dominated the pub, mingling with other frequenters, and for a time I didn't sense anything out of the ordinary. But about an hour into the party I felt a different kind of energy that didn't quite seem to fit the situation. At first I sensed a cool shaft of very fresh air (I am very sensitive to pure air, seeking it in our ongoing experiments). Then, I noticed a woman who stood out from the rest, I'd say of about 60 or so. I had never seen her before. She was dressed in a soft flowing lavender gown, had shining clear skin and kind but penetrating eyes that focused intensely on the people she spoke with. I was aware of her moving across the room chatting with people as she went. She was coming closer to me, although she did not seem in a rush to go anywhere.

I lost track of her, but when I moved to the bar to get another drink, I turned into her.

"Hello, Adderley. Seems like you have something great to celebrate."

"Thanks, I appreciate it. Do I know you? You know who I am, but who are you?"

She looked at me with a total and riveting attention. "I am Peneth, Peneth Tipton. I am an inventor and, well, a poet. I like to think of myself as a mentor. But that's not important. What's important is YOU. Congratulations!"

"Interesting name, Peneth. So, what are you doing here?"

"Actually I'm here to see you. You have a big transition ahead, and I'm interested in transitions. Think maybe I can help."

"Well, Peneth, my work is really technical and I doubt . . . ."

Peneth interrupted me, "A VP job is more than technical, isn't it, Adderley? That's why I want to suggest that you take some time to retreat and think about what you will become in this new role."

I must admit that I thought she was being a bit presumptuous and I wanted to get back to my party. "Thanks for your interest, but I generally avoid navel-gazing experiences."

"I understand," she said, all the time holding my gaze with her penetrating yet inviting stare. "All of this is a heady experience and there will be much to do. But...," and she handed me a card as she spoke, "...think about it. The LI Retreat Center is nearby and you will, I think, want to take advantage of what it offers."

Before I could respond, she smiled, nodded, and with a subtle flourish made her way through the pub crowd and out the door. I was about to toss the card in the nearby trashcan, but was interrupted by a colleague and slipped the now wrinkled card into my pocket.

CHAPTER 4
At Home

It was late when I got home and I felt very light-headed. I had scattered and uncomfortable thoughts about my "in-between" situation, feeling the weight of expectation deep in my chest, along with a creeping performance anxiety. But I also began to experience a warm swelling from a new sense of power and position.

I looked in the mirror and spoke to myself, "Vice President of Research and Development, Jada Division, BlythCo International—the company that would change the world and the vice president who would make sure it happened."

But even as I said this, I realized that I wasn't really confident that I could succeed in the job. In this moment of conundrum, the pressure in my chest increased and I felt dizzy. The face in the mirror went out of focus as, sweaty I... started... to loosen... my tie... Then, suddenly, darkness.

CHAPTER 5
The Dream

I am midway in my life's journey, lost in a dark and swampy forest. Others are here, must be here, but I can't see them. I hear sirens retreating into the distance. It's eerie. I must have strayed off a path, for I would not have deliberately chosen to enter this place. I thought there was a path. It is so dark, except for a faint and satiny light at the top of and behind what I think is a faraway mountain. I walk toward it, but I trip over exposed tree roots and the mountain eludes me. Ah, there is a gate and I think I see a road up the mountain. If only I can reach it.

I hear a muffled growl and shifting branches. A bear[ii] lumbers out, grizzled, menacing, staring at me with dripping fangs and blocking my way, ready to chase. I don't look directly at her, for fear of a challenge. Sidling to the right, I elude the bear but don't make any progress on the path.

Disoriented, I circle around, advancing, thickets all around until I see an opening. I trip and scramble towards it, when, dropping from the tree in front of me and hanging into the open space is a giant lizard[iii], muscular, eyes flashing red, tail wrapped tightly around a limb as thick as my waist. "No passage here," it seems to say. In my head reverberates, "There is no easy way for you... no easy way... no easy way." The reptile sways and glares, eyes twitching when I move, slowly now, backing up.

I fall into a shallow pit, check for anything broken and scramble out, hyperventilating. This is a fearful place, a disorienting place. Above me is a swirl of black, moving and pointed shadows –giant black birds, crows[iv] I think. They cackle ominously and obstruct my view above. I cover my head and eyes and stumble in a zigzag path to nowhere. I am lost and scared.

From another world, faintly at first, then so loud that it reverberates in shock through my body, I hear voices, and the humming of machines–a pump, I think.

"We're losing him..."

"One more time... one more..."

"Get ER ready..."

Something is covering my nose and mouth... For an instant I look back and forth into the faces of strangers and realize where I am, but the intensity of nearby light blinds me.

The Gateway

CHAPTER 6
The Surrender

Iawoke looking up at a blur of bottles and tubes and being wheeled down a long narrow hall. Someone put her hand on my shoulder, "Relax, we're going to get through it. Hang in there." Then, I was transported to another world. . .

I tried to focus, to comprehend what was happening. A waft of air swept past me, and with it a crumpled card with strange writing flitted briefly past. The letters on the card seemed to sparkle and I was drawn to them, feeling an overwhelming curiosity. "LI Retreat Center," it said.

I had lost my sense of time and was not sure how I got in front of a wood-planked door—one you might find in some medieval village. After a few seconds lightly touching it, I pressed the doorbell. The door creaked open and I took a deep breath and went in. Before I could change my mind, the door slammed closed and I was back in the forest of my dream. In the distance I heard the growl of a grizzly, the hiss of a lizard, and the cackles of crows. They created an invisible sound barrier that would not let me pass.

All of a sudden, Peneth appeared. She was dressed functionally in overalls and tall boots and carried a variety of tools in a waist belt. "Adderley. I knew you would return, for there are lessons here you must learn."

"Peneth, I don't really want to be here, but the door has disappeared, and the way out–that far away path to the light behind the mountain–is blocked and seems impassible. Can you help me get out of here?"

"I can't help you in the way you request, Adderley. I have a different mission," she said with a combination of authority and empathy in her voice. "The only way to reach that place you desire is to go away from it for now and learn the lessons of this place. Here you will face the shadow side of power so that you will know how to harness its energy.

"Power is a great gift. But the ability to wisely and consciously choose how to use it isn't yet fully in your reach. Part of you still acts from sleep or pressure or habit or without full regard for your power and the increasing impact of your choices.

"You may soon have too much institutional power *not* to become more wisely conscious. How you exercise that power has the potential for grave consequences, as you will see.

"Come with me."

We turned away from the mountain and faced in the direction that had been the retreat entrance. But the double doors had disappeared. Instead, in the distance we saw a giant and foreboding building. It was quite the opposite of the Jada headquarters. Rather it had the look of an old government or industrial building—boxy, uninviting, with dirty windows alternating with rusted metal plates. Smoke plumed out of seven rounded chimneys. The building was surrounded by a penitentiary-like wall topped with barbed wire that prevented a clear view of the lower levels of the building.

An owl sat on the roof, twisting its head fully round and back and showing large, yellow eyes that stopped momentarily to connect with my eyes. I had a hard time focusing on its eyes and was disturbed by my inability to focus. It was getting darker, even in this already dark place. As Peneth and I made our way through weeds and tangles, Peneth scythed a rough path with one of her tools. Nearing the wall I felt a bone-cutting chill.

CHAPTER 7
The Place of No Decision

A head was a large steel door in the wall. Tacked to it, a sign read, "If you enter, leave all hope behind."[v]

"Peneth, I'm not ready to do this. Bring me back to the entrance. If having additional power means I have to go into this place, I want to reconsider. I didn't sign up for this!"

As I spoke, the door opened and we were sucked into a crowd of people whose eyes looked like spinning spirals. They bumped into and tripped over each other, moving back and forth sideways. Their feet were calloused and dirty from the to and fro. For a time I bounced among them, caught up in the movement. Peneth stood fixed, watching me as people stepped around her.

Initially, I fought to move forward through the crowd, but I began to lose energy, engulfed in the side-to-side motion.

I heard Peneth's voice. "Adderley, these people have gifts that could make them leaders. They come from all centuries. They have refused to either respond to or reject the call to leadership and are forever stuck in their indecision. There is no hope for them, but for you . . . Yes."

She reached out to me. "Will you come with me to strengthen yourself for the leadership road ahead of you? Or will you join them here to neither experience the pain nor the joy of the full use of your gifts? Take my hand now and I'll guide you past this place of indecision."

I hesitated, my eyes beginning to spin, but ultimately I made a grand push through the crowd to join Peneth. She pulled me away from the crowd and into an eerie, twilight space that was still some distance from the building ahead. At this point I realized that the building was surrounded by a moat and not directly accessible. I could see the building's door but there was no land or bridge access.

As my eyes adjusted to the new light, I saw a large and surly crowd being told by someone dressed as an old sea captain[vi] to "Get in line!" The people grumbled, shouted, and pushed against and in front of each other to board a large raft being loaded at a small dock. With me in tow, Peneth cleared a path through the crowd.

"You know you can't bring him here, Peneth," rasped the Captain. "This place is for those already damned. It is for them to find and face, forever without hope, their eternal punishment. Move away."

Without flinching or raising her voice, Peneth responded, "Our mission is one over which you have no power, Captain. We are going to board. Make space."

Once we were on board and I had some sense of the situation, I bombarded Peneth with questions. "If I am not damned, why do you take me here? And if these horrible people are headed for eternal punishment, why do they scramble to make this crossing even as they scream and cry? I am totally confused and terrified, Peneth. I haven't fully decided to follow you, yet I'm here. What is this all about?"

"You will see, you will see. You *have* chosen even though you do not know and could not fully know what lies ahead. Your journey has begun."

At this point the raft lurched forward and we disappeared into an eerie fog. From an increasingly distant place, I heard Peneth speak to me in a fading whisper, "Relax, my friend, in this twilight hour before your journey. There is much to see and much to learn. You will need all of your energy to meet what lies ahead."

The Inferno

CHAPTER 8
First Circle: The Ignorant

I reached the other side of the moat, dimly aware of my river passage, and hearing a great metal door shut behind me. Peneth and I were in what appeared to be an enormous institutional reception area. To the left, a wall-size switchboard flashed hundreds of reddish-yellow lights—little flames. Ahead, a clock without hands sat above a sprawling, unattended olive-drab desk. Piles of resumés sat disheveled on the desk and floor. The heat was stifling even as our breaths were frosty mists. The top of an empty, smoke-filled glass elevator shaft poked out from the floor to the right, pulleys visibly moving and lifting or lowering something below. Muffled moans and shrieks and knocking sounds vibrated the elevator walls. My feet were scraped and hot within my shoes, for the floor was steaming. Peneth gestured towards a dark hallway between the reception desk and the sparking switchboard.

As we entered the hall, the heat lessened somewhat. Cries faded into the background and a cool yellow-orange light grew brighter ahead of us as we walked, leading us into a cafeteria-style space. There were no walls in sight. The place was enormous; endless in all directions. As I looked more closely I saw an expansive honeycomb of large plexi-glassed rooms, transparent but fixed and impermeable. Clusters of ghostly forms occupied each room and sat or stood around tables. They seemed neither in pain nor in joy.

Peneth put a name to the place. "Adderley, this is the First Circle of the Leadership Inferno. It is a kind of limbo, where residents neither experience pleasure nor pain. When alive, these people accepted formal leadership roles but used their positions and titles to expand their personal specialist skills. They did no real wrong, but were ignorant of the true potential and requirements of their leadership authority. They now remain forever cut off from larger impact and the satisfactions and rewards related to it.

"Look over there—that group talking so lively together! In life these people were terrific salespeople. But when they took on their formal leadership roles they used their management titles to sell more and to sell bigger. They amplified their own personal impact but didn't extend that beyond themselves to develop the institutions and people they led.

"And, see those beings just to the right of the sales group? They were all talented engineers and architects. They are still creating drawings, although they are frozen in the technologies they used in life. This is why some are using virtual reality design and others only T-squares. They used their positions to good technical ends and didn't get in the way of others' success, but they didn't help others excel as great designers and they didn't take on other, more expansive and integrative leadership responsibilities of their roles.

"The same is true for the cubicles here where the beings are doing financial calculations, or over there, creating service programs or teaching. All the ghosts here once held a formal management role at some level at some kind of institution. But they didn't learn about the different requirements of their leadership role, so they failed to deliver on their leadership responsibilities.

"These people never shifted their self-concept and behavior from being individual contributors to being people who create a performance environment and support for others—or whose job it was to build systems and processes bigger than themselves. So they missed an opportunity to have major ripple effects in the world, even though their personal contributions were stunning."

"This doesn't seem fair, Peneth," I said to her. "If they did no harm and made a personal difference, why are they in the Leadership Inferno at all? And how is it actually a punishment to be here? They don't seem to be in pain."

"Inferno is not just a state of inflicted pain, Adderley. It is also a state of loss. Those in this part of the Inferno will never experience the highest rewards for their gifts, for they stopped short of realizing the potential of their role. Imagine what could have happened if the great talents here had truly treated being a leader as a special vocation. When these people took on their formal leadership roles they became responsible for impacts bigger than themselves, not just *doing* the work themselves."

As she talked I had a fleeting thought about my recent action to take over our troubled research project—to *do* the work myself. I saw myself potentially in one of these cubicles, but before I could mine the implications, Peneth went on.

"In their lifetimes, these people accepted their leadership role, but they never really tried to understand what it required. It was their job to amplify, accelerate, support, focus, align, unleash, and develop all the resources around them. It was their job to reach across to people in other groups and roles and make links among groups. But they remained ignorant of these responsibilities. Now, they can't reach across to each other. They can't do the one plus one equals three magic that is part of real leadership, for they are unable to create anything new or see anything come to a new synthesis. Their reach is limited to these transparent but narrow personal skill cubicles in which they will forever live and work.

"You are right that they are somewhat content doing what they always loved. But watch how frequently and wistfully they look beyond their limited space to find what could have been.

"They are in the Circle of Ignorance. Don't let this be your lot, Adderley. If you truly decide to accept the new vice president role, then become fully aware of your new responsibilities and redefine your view of yourself as the leader your role requires. Ignorance of what you are taking on is not a defense when you are called to account."

"As we move through the most punishing parts of the Leadership Inferno, Adderley, know that accepting a formal leadership role obligates you to something bigger than just being a super 'you.' If this is *not* your vocation–your calling–find something else to do with your life or you will find yourself back here someday to reside in this terrible place forever. And you will miss out on the great satisfactions and rewards that come from doing good work in the world, whether as a formal leader or in another role of your choice."

At that point, we wound our way between the honeycombed cubicles, observing the ghostly forms there, and then we disappeared into a darkness that began to envelop us.

The Lesson: Be a leader who is AWARE of the requirements of formal leadership.

CHAPTER 9
Second Circle:
The Myopics

We left the limbo of ignorance and stepped back into the heat that seemed to be the soul of this place. Slime-green walls were everywhere. A terrible screech invaded as if from ten thousand fingernails on a chalkboard. The glass elevator rose to meet us. Its operator was a deformed creature wearing a heavy steel coat. He dripped sweat from the intense heat of the elevator's shaft. The door opened and he spun the rotating elevator control with a ferocious whirl. However, only the lever moved, for he had disengaged it from the fulcrum.

He looked at us with murderous red-green eyes as Peneth spoke. "Minos[vii], you will not spin this man into any permanent home in hell. He is in my charge and travels here on behalf of many above. Take us down one level and leave us to our task."

"You know that I am the Judge, Peneth. It is my job, not yours, to decide to which level I will take those who pass here, even though by their deeds they have made the choice that I only execute. How dare you tell me where to go." He paused as his face took on a deferential look. "AAGHKK! This once I will do as you ask, for there may be promise in this one, even though I see in him already the stain of chances lost, decisions ill-made, offenses that may bring him back forever and irrevocably to me and the justice I wield."

The elevator ride seemed endless. As we descended there was only blackness and searing heat—then a noise of wind as if from an increasingly narrow tunnel.

The doors opened and we were tossed into a terrible storm of hot rain and tornado-like winds. There was something in the distance calling us to refuge, but the call was faint. Peneth grabbed me and we each tethered ourselves to individual ropes that were anchored somewhere, where I could not see. As we hung onto the ropes and swung in the wind, we saw that people of all shapes and sizes were being blown in all directions as the wind continually shifted.

Several reached for spectacles, crying out that they could not see beyond their noses. Others were getting sick from the buffeting and couldn't stop retching.

Peneth spoke to me as we dangled in the storm. "Adderley, this is the place where people who were formal leaders are punished for their short-term and myopic decisions. Over there are thousands who sold out the future of their organizations in order to achieve short-term ends. They also failed to lift themselves above the issues of the day to see the big picture around the decisions they were making. They will forever be unable to see anything in the distance or to see the bigger picture because that was the choice they made in life. Others, in a peculiar twist, will never be able to see what is nearby. In both cases, the short and long term, the pieces and the whole will never come together for them."

At this point, there was a lull in the winds. In the opening we saw hundreds of overstuffed people sitting in mud. They were dressed in the business attire of many countries. Currency notes of all kinds overflowed from bowls in front of them and dribbled from their mouths; they seemed incapable of stopping their eating frenzy.

I let go of my support rope in this wind hiatus, dropped to the ground and approached one of the wallowing souls: "Why are you doing this? Who are you and what got you here?"

"My name is Mufti. In my life as a manager I put short-term success first. That wasn't always bad, but I know that over the years we could have done a lot better if I had thought more about the bigger picture and longer term. Now it's my lot to eat the short-term profits we made while my body's overall health suffers eternally. There are lots of people like me from companies here, but it's not only business leaders here. We always get the blame. Go see what you find over there . . . lots of union leaders, elected government officials, and even goody-goody people from the non-profits. Hah! We are all the same – looking for instant gratification and the easy solution."

Peneth watched me from her rope perch as I slogged through the hot muck to a pit where hundreds were being pelted with an endless assortment of objects.

I asked no one in particular, "What is happening here? What did you do to deserve this treatment?"

Heads turned to each other in obvious shame. One woman, dressed in formal attire, answered. "I was a congresswoman in life. Again and again I was re-elected, but looking back, I accomplished little for my people and my country. I was too busy diverting funds to pet projects that could get me re-elected but, if I had looked more broadly, I should not have supported. It was good while it lasted and kept me in power. My projects even met a few needs. But now I am paying for short-term thinking that created many longer-term problems and that really wasn't in the deeper best interest of the people I was supposed to serve. I'm being pelted with the very projects I supported because of my selfishness and short-sightedness."

At this point a pork bone grazed the side of her head and she couldn't continue speaking.

As I maneuvered back toward Peneth, something grabbed my ankle. I fell and found myself face-to-face with a blind man who was trying to grab spectacles that were just beyond his reach.

"Hey. I'm Ripley, one of the most powerful union stewards in my institution. I don't belong here. You've got to get me out. I was a man of the people. I really showed those maggot corporates what it means to cross swords with the people. We squeezed every dime we could out of those fat cats. Sure my cronies and I got part of that, but that's no crime. The bankruptcies weren't my fault; bad leadership, that was it."

His grip on my ankle hurt. "Let me go. It sounds like you were all in it together. I only hope there is time for me... to..."

The wind resurged, creating an opening in the fog. I jumped up to catch a rope just in time to see the opening close. I was picked up by the increasing wind and watched the swirling, groping bodies resume their endlessly buffeted existence as they faded into the mist.

We swung into a fixed position at the end of our taut tethers, and Peneth spoke. "Adderley, what is the lesson you learn in this second circle of the Leadership Inferno?"

"I wonder, Peneth, what it is that causes us to want gratification now rather than later? It seems much easier to go for short-term benefit and reward than to sacrifice now for results later."

I stopped talking for a minute so I could think. Peneth didn't interrupt my silence. I realized how tricky it is to sort out short-term pressures and then thought out loud. "Even though we know that some things that feel good today will create problems for us tomorrow, it is really tough to use willpower and salesmanship for the longer-term best interest. The whole world seems to collude that both we and the people we serve want things now, not later. The media, shareholders, citizens, and others care mainly about what is happening now and how fast their current desires can be satisfied. We face impatient investors and demanding customers and citizens. It's hard for a leader to stand firm for short-term sacrifices or even to spend more than ten minutes focused on any one issue! And if we are able to focus on the long-term for longer than that, we still have to stay alive and in business in the short-term. These are not easy matters."

I realized that what I saw in this circle was a lesson about keeping both the short- and the long-term in mind and standing up for the long-term as well as the short. "If leaders can't do this, then who will?" I said to myself, realizing that I'd been drifting into that instant gratification place a lot lately.

Then we were sucked back into Minos' elevator.

Minos, with an increasingly intense and burning glare sputtered, "Here we go to Circle Three."

The Lesson: Be a BIFOCAL leader who sees the short and long term, the local and the global picture.

CHAPTER 10
Third Circle: The Reductionists

Minos put the elevator control in gear, swinging the lever to the third level. As he did so and the elevator lurched into another descent, he bellowed an earth-shaking guffaw. "I love these sins that only humans can commit. I will never be out of work here. HA!!!"

The heat and ominous aura intensified as we seemed to hurtle through space. The entire elevator opened and a strange world appeared, divided in two. On the left side were angular, geometric caricatures of people, Picasso-esque forms. In the distance on the right, but beyond a passage, were blindingly colorful and somewhat ethereal floating organic forms that I couldn't identify.

Peneth dragged me to the left. As we entered that space, all color disappeared and we were in a world of stark black and white. Everything appeared stenciled.

A guard desk blocked our easy passage. The woman staffing it wore a police hat and, facing down with only the top of her hat in sight, was stamping some papers. When she looked up, I was shocked. The right side of her face was missing and her brain was visible on the other side. It was a frightening sight.

She pounded on a huge ring binder topped with papers. "What do you want here? You may not pass without completing these forms and agreeing to follow the procedures in this manual."

As I moved towards her, I tripped over what appeared to be an unfinished puzzle made up of angular pieces and layers. On closer look, it was fragments of a person.

The piece with the mouth moved, but was constrained and stated with difficulty, "All my life I played by the rules. Rules and procedures were in charge: I made sure they were followed to a 'T.' I was a mouthpiece for the institution, the gatekeeper for everything. They called me a bureaucrat and I was proud of that, for nobody and no issue were exempt from following the procedures. How else can any organization operate? When people think and make exceptions, things fall apart. We need tight control–procedures, policies must rule. People must stick to their roles and authorized communication channels. When people think outside of the box there is chaos. My job was to prevent chaos."

At this point, the guard kicked the speaking puzzle. "Fragment, you know the rules here. You may not speak without permission. Get back behind me and mind your business."

Peneth pulled me past the guard. "There is more to learn and see here than from these fragments and from you, guard. I have a document that gives us free access. Let us through."

After scrutinizing Peneth's pass, the guard grumbled but moved out of the way.

We slipped into a world of half-brained people like the guard. They were all working on charts, graphs, and analyses of one kind or another. Seminars were taking place everywhere. One was called "How to Break Things Down to Build Them Up." There was another with the topic, "How to Construct Team Spirit." Others included, "The Organization Structure that Solves all Problems," "Get the Behavior You Want by Manipulating Rewards," "Ultra-rational Problem-solving and Decision-making." There was even one titled, "Analyzing Your Way Out of the Inferno."

In all seminar rooms these half-headed shadows of people busily gathered around seemingly endless white boards with equations, lists, and decision diagrams. Many perpetually scratched what was left of their heads. There were big jars of pain pills everywhere, with some ghosts moaning while they pressed their heads in their hands, saying they couldn't stand the pain. Periodically someone said, "But something is missing, something is missing. We don't have the full picture."

I turned to Peneth. "I am confused about the message here. These shadows are using their brains to organize things and to think problems through. Isn't that noble? Isn't rationality one of our biggest strengths? Isn't it the leader's job to analyze and solve problems? Why is this an infraction that brings people to this place and dooms them to an endlessly painful existence?

Peneth responded, "Before I help you to see what is happening here, Adderley, let's slip to the other side of this Third Circle, for only then will you have the full story."

Moving past the guard and the endless stash of angular puzzle people in various stages of fragmentation, we entered a bizarre long and narrow hall full of disconnected hoses, cables, wires, and plugs. The black and white morphed into greys and then I realized that the ends of some of the cables and wires were sparking and sizzling, creating flashes of blue, green, yellow, and red. As my eyes grew accustomed to the eerie and intermittent light from these sparks, I saw that behind us was a wall of broken plugs and connections–the spokes of the connections were missing outlets to plug into. But even if there were outlets, these plugs were rusted, cracked, and jagged and wouldn't be functional.

After a seeming eternity of climbing over cables and jumping away from erratic lightning flashes from rogue, disconnected wires, I saw something looming ahead. There seemed to be a series of tunnels and holes of various sizes and shapes. Rainbow-colored flashes sprang from deep within them, but they were not inviting. I swallowed my fear and headed toward a tunnel that looked like a passageway.

"Adderley, don't be lured into the abyss through that tunnel. You'll never return. Come with me this way." Peneth pulled me back, leading me to the right and toward a newly visible sliding door.

We walked through an open door into a weird scene of mesmerizing color and floating organic shapes. It was so different from the black and white, clearly-defined space on the other side of the cable hall that I was more confused than ever about how they could be part of the same Inferno circle. It made no sense.

As I tried to focus, something spoke to me out of a place that I couldn't fully reach with my senses. It was a feeling from somewhere and nowhere at the same time. "I am an idea, a possibility, a creative thought looking for a place to land. Grab me and bring me to life, for I can only wander in this never-place until something brings me into existence and gives me shape and purpose."

From elsewhere, a dream. "No, take me! I was the leader who recognized the learning that almost happened and that could have changed the direction of things. But I had disdain for plans and discipline. Grab me and make me real, if only for a minute so I can experience myself as more than a potentiality."

And from another direction, an intuition. "I sponsored a breakthrough idea that could have changed the course of bankruptcies and mismanagements. But the idea was only part of the solution and I left it for a new thought before the idea could take root. So I am doomed now to never see an idea realized, to always roam as a thought and a potentiality that never comes to fruition."

The inchoate pressures around us generated more angst and heat than I had yet experienced. I was surrounded by colors and energies, some of which I couldn't see, hear, feel, taste, or smell. But they crushed me from all directions. I felt that I was running everywhere at once until I felt myself pulled back into the hall of disconnected but flashing cables, Peneth propelling me towards a spot that the autonomous jumping cords couldn't reach for the moment.

Peneth said, "We're going to sit here for a few minutes in the connecting space that both sides of this Inferno circle would seek to repair—for this connecting space is broken, as you can see. Because it is broken, the left and right side processes are running amuck on their own, forever disconnected from each other. Adderley, leaders must draw on the full and diverse capabilities of their own and others' brains—both sides, all faculties. Otherwise the solutions they sponsor and the decisions they make will not and cannot match the complexities they and their organizations face."

She stopped talking for a moment while we both looked around this place. I thought about the lessons presented in this circle. On the left side I'd seen the extreme of the brain's ability to think rationally–to create step-by-step plans, solve problems analytically, and to keep actions on a directed path. The equipment for these rational abilities is located on the left side of most peoples' brains.

Then my thoughts shifted to the other side, the place of the amazing creative and emotional capabilities—where intuitive, discontinuous, feeling processes seemed to float and ignite in their own time horizon without conscious thought or planning.

"Adderley, occasionally some from the left and right sides of this circle will escape into this connecting hall to repair the damage and reconnect things. These temporary escapees are the lost souls who realize that there is something missing that, if recovered, could make them whole and end their suffering. You heard them speak. But as you can see, the connecters in this part of the Third Circle are damaged beyond repair."

I picked up on her stream of thought as I realized the implications. "So the leaders in this circle will forever only be either rational or intuitive in their approach to what is around them, to the problems and opportunities that require both parts of the brain."

I realized that the people here will be forever reductionist in their approach. They will never be able to bring the rational and intuitive together. I slumped into deep thought, examining my own way of approaching problems. I knew I had been guilty of this kind of splitting off of my and others' full brainpower and I wondered what it had cost me, others, and Jada. I imagined the rational and creative parts of my and others' brains working together in synergy, and was glad I still had the ability to be a catalyst for this integration.

Peneth let me think about this for a while.

The Lesson: Be a leader who is SYNERGISTIC—
including diverse thoughts, interactions,
and perspectives.

CHAPTER 11
Fourth Circle: The Abdicators

There was a clanging sound in the distance and an ear-splitting screech. The elevator was back. Minos lumbered out, red eyes glaring until they rested on me, prickling my skin. Peneth stepped in front of me and we climbed over stray wires and cords, jumping away from sparks on our way to the elevator.

"Adderley, we have to move on for the time we are allotted is short," Peneth said.

As we descended, the elevator shook violently from side to side. At times it seemed to go up and then down. The eerie red glow was punctuated by leaping flashes of yellow-green flames seeping through the joints. It seemed that there was no real direction or destination. Even

Minos appeared more disturbed than usual. I dreaded the next part of this drama and felt a real angst somewhere deep in my psyche.

The door opened to what I thought was a construction site, but there was havoc, and danger seemed to lurk everywhere—hung heavy in the air in the form of muffled snorts and cries and odors of things decaying or rusting. People near to us were yelling at each other. Half-paved roads, badly graveled paths, broken-slatted walkways, and foot-trampled narrow patches of dying grass spread out in a variety of directions. But all of them suddenly ended without connecting to each other.

Signs lay scattered around. They said, "This way" but pointed every which way. Strange pieces of equipment dotted the landscape. They clearly couldn't function; some had odd numbers of wheels that were all trying to move away from each other. Others were rigged with contorted chains and pulleys in tugs of war with themselves. An assortment of vision-blockers—slime, posters, cakes of mud—covered the vehicles' windows.

Far out in the distance, undulating ribbons of some kind of mass flooded towards us from all sides, a pincer effect. What appeared to be flying creatures hovered over the front edges of the converging masses. Dark and jagged clouds raced back and forth through the sky like huge and ill-coordinated bombers.

The scraggly path we were on shook and rippled, propelling us forward against our wishes, for my intent was to run back to the elevator and put myself at the mercy of Minos to take me anywhere but here. As I was shaken forward, my feet seemed to stick at each step, as if they were suction cups wanting me to stay put. At one particularly sticky step, I fell to the ground and pulled hard on my now-glued shoe.

The path, pulling harder on my shoe, came alive and spoke. "You! Adderley, I recognize you! I am Edward West, the dean of the university engineering department where you taught environmental design. That was before you went on to your lucrative corporate life and started on the path to your own corruption. I'm glad to see you are falling into my path. If I am to suffer here, then I want to take others like you with me."

"I know you," I said. "How I remember you! You had everything going for you at old Mater: new department, some good initial endowments, everything. And you threw it all away. There was no direction for our department and nobody to market us or build the university or the partnerships that we needed for real success. We attracted great engineering and scientific minds, but it was everyone for him or herself. Some of our worst instructors thrived, spending the least time possible with us so they could take lucrative consulting jobs. There was no accountability and a terrible cutthroat atmosphere. When the university went through those tough economic periods, you didn't speak up for us. You said it was up to the finance department to make things work. We were a leaderless ship on a stormy sea. Even when we seemed to agree on a larger direction, you lost interest and didn't follow through. Because of you, I left dispirited!"

"Be careful not to judge too harshly," Edward replied. I can see by your aura that these are familiar behaviors for you. Stay and keep me company here." The tug on my foot increased and my foot began to disappear into the path.

Thankfully, Peneth reached into the sinkhole. Her hand created a release reaction and the path collapsed into stillness. My foot came out of my shoe as she spoke. "Listen well, Adderley. Observe what you see here and be careful about these temptations to which you are easily prone."

We moved quickly, jumping off and between the disconnected paths. We came to a slight ridge, climbing down through an intermittent fog. We were now in a shallow but expansive valley. Huge crews in identical work clothes worked robotically, hammering and nailing and gluing a seemingly infinite number of giant, miles-long prefabricated buildings. The people and the buildings all looked the same, and there was no joy, no emotion at all in the doing. The crews' movements were jerky as though in pantomime.

Too far away for me to decipher them, hundreds of objects bounced like jumping beans. Peneth led us toward them.

"Peneth, what is this place? Who lives here?"

As I asked this, I noticed that the jumping beans had formed queues that were snaking toward the ends of the prefabricated buildings.

Loud voices came from the queue: "No, not that way! That is not the right way. This will not take us there. I will not submit to this."

In the midst of and around what was becoming a terrible refrain, I heard thwacks and hissing sounds of whips. The jumping beans grew larger as we got closer to them. They shape-shifted into angry men and women of all contours, sizes, and colors. They writhed under the slash of the whips while simultaneously crying out and looking fearfully behind them toward the horizon at what I then realized was an advancing and angry mob.

Those in the queue could not step out of the line. They marched inexorably into openings at the ends of the prefabricated buildings. Once in, they slid on conveyor belts, visible intermittently through narrow windows. Along the way they turned once again into bean-shaped figures, all alike.

Peneth stepped between one of the queues and the guard who was keeping it in order. This gave me a chance to talk with one of those in the queue. I asked him, "Who are you? What did you do to deserve this?"

He responded, "I am now only known as 'Beanly.' In my Earth life I was a manager in a big government agency. My crime was abdication. Like others who were leaders in businesses, non-profits, churches, all kinds of organizations, I abandoned important parts of my leadership role. The sin of abdication is not limited to any one kind of institution. All of us here were paid in money or prestige to lead. It was our job to make sure that our organizations had the best leaders and leadership processes and systems.

"We knew that it was our job to make sure that there was life and energy from top to bottom in our institutions." He spoke while sweating profusely and wiping his forehead with a dingy blue and yellow striped cloth.

"But we were lazy or unwilling to do the work we were paid to do," he went on. "Instead we delegated too much of the important leadership work to administrative staff and expected processes and procedures to operate without our involvement. We expected others to communicate for us, to manage tough problems and conflicts, to deliver difficult messages. Often we expected others to follow rules and procedures that we didn't follow ourselves. In the process, we turned what was in our care into lifeless systems that lacked credibility. We turned great people like those in human resources or finance departments into robots and bureaucratic enforcers of the approaches that were ours to infuse with life."

"I don't understand," I said. "What is happening here then, and how does this punishment fit?"

Beanly responded, "We now live forever in the situations we created for others. In my pocket on the back of my shirt are the communications and leadership actions I wish I had implemented when I had the chance. But I can't access them and I have no power to implement them here. No power. My own awareness and lost power continually burn and taunt me. And now I am about to enter, for the many thousandth time, the dehumanizing cookie-cutter process that will form me for my next round of the same endless process. You know what I mean? Imagine continually cycling through reams of performance management or budgeting steps. Imagine endlessly playing the games that allow us to tick off the boxes showing that 'we did this,' knowing that we treated important leadership responsibilities as bureaucratic burdens.

"I've said enough. I have made my bed, and must now lie in it."

I wanted to hear more. "Wait, I still don't..."

At this point, the guard shoved Beanly into the end of one of the many look-alike, ticky-tacky buildings. Stepping back, I spotted a bean-like figure as it slid past the first window. I thought I recognized the small blue and yellow striped splotch of Beanly's handkerchief as the figure passed.

I wanted to follow him to the end of the production line. There was more to learn about abdicating important leadership work to others. But I was interrupted by a rumbling of earthquake proportions. The fog had lifted in this valley, but the storm clouds were coalescing and huge vulture-like birds were swarming like bees in the distance. The moving mass neared from what I think was the West. It was angry. It was alive. It was a shouting mob.

"Down with the Abdicators. We gave them our time. We gave them our skills. We gave them our lives, our careers. They failed us. Down with them," the mob chanted. "Let them feel the brunt of our power even as they abdicated theirs."

I looked about frantically for a way to escape and climb back up out of the valley. I didn't know where Peneth was. All around me were ghoulish forms. It seemed that the many paths to nowhere were flexing and I saw that they were actually made of flattened human bodies. They appeared to be mustering every energy, every power, every muscle to shift into a more mobile form so they could run away. Some were successful enough to begin to run, but I could see that the situation was hopeless for them.

The swelling mob flooded menacingly forward. As it surged, a spokesperson for the mob rose, lifted above and carried along the surge.

He spoke. "Hear me all you who abdicated your gift of power. You evaded your role. We, your followers, agreed to bring our special skills in order to create something together that we couldn't do alone–great products, services for others, buildings, crops, governments, roads, churches, knowledge, tools to help us and humanity and the world itself develop and grow. We joined you so we could be in an organization–a community–with common visions, common goals, common interests. But you let us down.

"We were bodies, lungs, and bones. You were supposed to be the heart, nervous tissue, and connections. That connectivity and coordination were your role, and you delegated it to others or treated it as an after-thought while you enjoyed the fruits of your position.

"We know that we are culpable, too. We are in this dreadful place because we allowed you to abdicate. We followed without you leading. You were chosen. You had disproportionate power, and you let us down. When you didn't lead, we blamed you and each other, accepting things as they were.

"Now you will feel all of our power. We will show you the true weight and heft of the crowd and of the power you chose not to exercise. And we will suffer with you for our part in that infernal play."

At this point, the mob became a raging molten mass, heavy as rock, hot as lava. It flattened everything in front of it. When it came to me, there was a blinding blast of lightning from the now completely joined, jagged clouds as they turned everything around us pitch black.

A whisper immediately after the flash spoke to me. "Something of you, part of you remains behind. Run quickly or you will never leave."

I tripped in the dark, hyperventilating and heart pounding. When my eyes adjusted, I felt my feet, one bare, walking on hot tar. The only object in sight was a small cubed piece of a building that seemed to be part of one of the prefabricated concoctions we saw in the valley. I sat on it to cool my feet, and Peneth and I talked about what we had seen.

"There was an extra level of pull for you to this circle, Adderley. Do you know what that was all about?"

"Peneth, there is too much to absorb here. Meeting my former mentor, well, I see I have been prone to some of his failures. I must admit that I have avoided some of the leadership work that the people in this circle also avoided. I've let staff handle things I should have. In fact just before I got word of my promotion, I was about let someone in Human Resources take charge of a conversation that I should have had myself. And I must admit that I really don't put much leadership energy into things like budgets and plans. Most of the time I just try to work around them instead of making them work better. Maybe that's why they don't really carry much weight with my teams. But I need more time to absorb all this!"

Peneth nodded and left me to my thoughts.

The Lesson: Be a Leader who is
ACCOUNTABLE for and brings life into all aspects of
the leadership function.

CHAPTER 12
Fifth Circle:
The Cowards

After some time passed, I noticed that Peneth had moved on. I limped away from the madness of the Fourth Circle, trying to catch up with her. The terrain had transformed itself and we walked for a long time on a hot, paved surface. In order to minimize the burn, I lifted my heel, walking on the ball of my bare foot. This created an odd walk-jump gait. I wasn't sure where the elevator was or if we were headed toward it.

"When I visit this place, I often wonder why anyone would want to be a formal leader," Peneth told me. Why would anyone want to take on such a difficult role that carries the potential for so much harm? The power is attractive, I guess. Also, I'm sure that most people have good intentions. How many actually live those intentions? Well there is a danger of power corrupting, isn't there, Adderley?"

"I wasn't aware that there were so many potential pitfalls and shadow paths for leaders, Peneth," I responded. It's sobering and..."

Before I could finish my sentence, I heard the clatter of pulleys that I now knew signaled Minos'–and the elevator's–arrival. I hopped and limped faster, for I could feel my bare foot swelling. We entered a dusty area and through the smog I saw the now familiar doors opening. A sound of commotion, of people talking all at once, bounced off the elevator walls. He closed the door and we careened, faster than before, deep into the bowels of the Inferno building. I saw the control lever swing to "Level 5." It seemed to take forever to reach that floor. The commotion grew louder and was ear-shattering.

What awaited was frightening. It had all the worst features of a haunted house, Halloween, and the most sinister marsh. Resonating roars as from lions shook the earth. Gigantic insects–spiders and crickets the size of horses–prowled at the edge of a boggy area. Shades of people moved in tandem, some of them engaged in constant loud chatter that seemed to hurt their own ears, for they covered them and shook their heads as they continually talked. At the same time, they looked furtively and fearfully around, jumping in fright at every roar or chatter of the giant insects.

One voice stood out. "I am Arthur. I *am* speaking up. I *am* talking. I can't stop talking even though my throat is in constant pain. I must rest it, must rest it, but I can't control my own voice," the voice said.

I followed the voice and saw a figure grabbing his own throat as though trying to choke himself.

He continued, "I *am* speaking up! I *am* talking! I can't stop talking! My throat is in constant pain! I must rest it, must rest!" he screamed as a huge spider blocked his path, ready to pounce. "Don't come after me, don't hurt me! I *am* speaking up! I *am* talking!"

Behind him I saw a giant web. Thousands were caught in it, all constantly talking in a manner similar to Arthur, as huge spiders crawled around and over them. It was a horrible sight and the human flies writhed in anguish.

"This fifth circle is for cowards, Adderley," Peneth said. "Here you will find people who had the power of position but didn't have the courage to use it in difficult situations. They took the easy way out to avoid conflict. They looked away when they saw bad decisions and even wrongdoing. They failed to defend and represent the people they led or the larger purposes they served. They kept quiet and now suffer by never again experiencing quiet. They didn't surmount their fears of speaking up and now suffer by living in constant fear. But that's not all that is punished here. There are other types of cowardice!"

We brushed away cobweb residue, moving deeper into the eerie landscape, ghouls floating by. I had never felt so afraid. My fear was raw, reaching like claws through my bones and bowels. Way off in the distance a part of the sky was blood red. We were heading toward it. The atmosphere was tangible and seemed to be walking through me, amplifying my own fear. If I had a measuring device for it, I would say that what I felt was more than a hundred times more frightening than anything I'd faced in the living world.

We drew closer to the reddened sky and what appeared to be a huge bonfire, red hot. Nearing it, the heat further inflamed my fear. I was sweating and wondered how long my own moisture supply would last. I thought I would burst from the searing energy in and around me. Peneth placed a cool hand on my forehead and beckoned me on. I could hardly breathe. And then I saw it. Too many bodies to count, sitting in the fire, blackened from the flames.

"If only I'd had the guts to face into those conflicts and understand what was behind them. It was my job to bring people together," a male voice said. "But I couldn't stand the heat and they all ended up fighting and working against each other when they could have, should have, come together. My job, my job, my role. I let them destroy each other. Now it's my fate to sit perpetually in flames. Oh, that I had faced what wasn't comfortable when I had a chance to be the leader I was paid to be!"

A female voice spoke up. "I couldn't stand conflict; walked away from it. I made sure that people kept conflict away from me when what we needed was a good airing of ideas–listening until we understood and could see all the views. Eventually it was easier to simply have people who were 'just like me' around me; 'Yes, Ma'am' people. They tell me this is what killed our company. We just didn't see the competition coming and the markets changing. A pure and simple case of cowardice."

Flames swallowed her as she spoke. There was a terrible and lingering scream.

"Adderley," Peneth said, "money and prestige and position come with your leadership role, but with this power comes added responsibilities that may not be comfortable. The people in this circle shied away from the confrontational and difficult parts of their job, the parts requiring courageous action. They refused to face tough and uncomfortable situations where they might have run counter to those with more power than they had. They..."

As she spoke, a regiment of what appeared to be soldiers marched past the huge bonfire, knocking me to the ground and almost trampling me. Peneth pulled a long-handled hammer out of her tool belt, extending the hammerhead for me to grab so she could pull me out of the way.

These people all appeared to be officers, but they were marching as though they were infantry. As they marched, their clothing changed – first Navy garb, then Army, then Air Force, then Special Forces. All uniforms were clearly very tight, making it hard to breathe. They were all bare-footed, with bruised skin on their feet, and obviously in severe pain.

I ran to keep up with them. "Where are you going? Why do you march?"

A very tired man with two stars of a general answered. "We march towards dreams we will never realize," he said, "and toward a certain death, only to resurrect and repeat the journey without arriving at a destination. For we in this platoon were strategists in life, but we could not take the tough actions to make the strategies live. We didn't have the guts to stand firm for the new directions and changes we knew were needed. We gave speeches about the future. We talked about new visions and sold many others on new dreams. But we waffled in the face of political forces and resistance. We couldn't put ourselves out there for what we knew was right and what couldn't come alive without us. We created expectations and then let them be dashed to the ground. Because of us, the whole idea of 'leader' lost its luster. People lost confidence."

"I sent other people out there to fight while I hung back," confessed the man next to him, a sergeant. "I don't know how many of my troops I left hung out to dry. When Minos told me my fate was Circle Five, I instantly knew it was the right place even as I shuddered in a shake more horrific than death. I was a coward in my life and I let down the many people I led. I let them all down because I wasn't willing to put myself out there."

I was confused. "But how does your punishment fit your crime? I don't see it!"

Peneth gave me my answer. "Adderley, these people march continuously without ever getting to a new place, even though they know where they want to be. They walk only in old formations and in old directions, never finding a new way. They see where they want to go, but because they would not stand firm and persist through uncertainty and challenge as leaders in life and during the chaotic periods that are part of new directions, they will never see any promised land. And this is pure torture, for they are capable of dreaming big dreams and envisioning other ways. And they know and are conscious of their sins and their loss."

I was struck by the magnitude of what they had lost and by the awareness of the leadership legacy they left behind. I felt a deep and inconsolable anguish just as the marching strategists accelerated their pace, kicking up a storm of hot dust and insects.

All around us were harsh whispers and screams, – cavernous roars of, "Cowards! Cowards!! Cowards!!! COWARDS!!!!"

I pushed my palms against my ears but couldn't escape the searing sound and the stomach-splitting fear. I was caught up in a tornado of noise and was hurled somewhere. As I whirled, my history as a formal leader–team leader, supervisor, manager–passed before me. I saw the times I had failed to speak up for what I thought was right or to support the people I was leading. I tried to remember the big visions we pursued and wondered if I had been courageous enough in standing up for them.

While I didn't feel I belonged in this circle, I understood the temptations. Something inside me woke up and I realized that my courage as a leader is important, no matter how personally traumatic the situation might be.

The Lesson: Be a leader who is COURAGEOUS in the face of conflict, challenge, and uncertainty.

CHAPTER 13
Sixth Circle:
Abusers of Rank

There was a loud ringing in my ears and I felt unable to move, as though wrapped in cellophane. Vaguely aware of a kind of super-sonic descent, my stomach in my throat, I felt part of an avalanche or earthquake, rapidly falling, slipping, sliding. A swirl of images swung clockwise around me. Minos' face and penetrating eyes appeared fleetingly in various stages of glare. Peneth, too. I was aware that she was nearby but it was a feeling and I couldn't see her.

I heard a loud thump and bounced violently.

"This is as far as I can take you without you being here for cause and forever," Minos informed me.

The elevator opened into what seemed to be an antechamber to an underground vault. Something resonated—a fleeting image. But the vault was in the distance and was heavily guarded by agitated, big-fanged dogs straining mightily at their leashes.

"We're approaching the core of the Leadership Inferno and won't pass into or out of it easily or without pain," said Peneth." I will try my best to lead us through, but I've requested additional help from those more powerful than I."

At that moment there was a violent commotion near the vault door. Three winged and shrouded creatures[viii], half bird, half human, descended, further agitating the guard dogs. The creatures cackled a challenge.

The creatures cackled a challenge. "In the last centuries we, the Furies, welcomed the darkest shadows of self-absorbed regulators, tax officials, and investment managers. As their mouthpieces and standing in for the evil Archangel himself, we will not let you violate a space that their dark sides have helped shape and maintain. Beyond this door you may not go, for it is under our control. Do not disturb."

At that point I heard the Furies utter what sounded like a curse or spell.

"Let all the consciously destructive forces of the universe converge here to stop this invasion by those who would rob us of our worldly servants. Sister Medusa[ix], whose stare will turn this intruder into stone and prevent him from returning to Earth as our enemy, we conjure you to work with us and stop his passing. Freeze him forever in space and time as our eternal prisoner!"

I hadn't read a lot of classical mythology, but I knew that Medusa meant big trouble! I felt a surge of hot wind.

"We are moving into the grips of much more powerful forces, Adderley, "Peneth explained. "Turn away from the vault."

She put her hands over my eyes and wouldn't let go for an interminable period (Minutes? Months? Years? Eons?). I had an irresistible temptation to take a quick peek. Hazy thoughts of Lot's wife and Sodom and Gomorrah mingled. Peneth cried out to something or someone to help us.

The hot winds suddenly shifted, and a cool spring-like breeze enveloped us. A brief brush of something fragrant passed by. The dogs quieted down. Peneth released her tight hold over my eyes. The Furies had disappeared and the vault door opened. We rushed through, facing the top of what seemed to be an endless spiral staircase. Everything below glowed red—an intense heat verging on purple.

Peneth spoke. "An emissary from the virtuous side of power[x] has just helped us to pass. But hurry. We must climb into the next circle before the immense opposition we just faced reassembles itself. Come."

We scrambled down the stairs. A noxious, rotting smell assaulted us and I stepped back up several spirals to find a way to breathe and to clear my stinging eyes.

"We must move on, Adderley," Peneth warned. "The only way out is down. Strengthen yourself to absorb what you experience here so that you can return to the world with the awareness of the shadow side that is essential to your full power. What lies ahead will not be easy. Stay close."

We continued winding down the stairway, arriving in a place that appeared to be totally surrounded by an open and flooded sewage trench. A hot red rain plopped steaming spiral whorls into the festering conduit and lapped the edges of the island it isolated.

"That is our next destination. It is the Isle of Those Who Abuse Rank. There you will meet those who willfully and shamelessly used their formal power to diminish, subdue, intimidate, and even enslave others while lifting themselves up. It will not be possible for you to imagine the pain of their punishments, for part of their curse is to feel suffering at superhuman levels. This is because they have deliberately used their power in ways that created pain and suffering for and interfered with the growth of others."

At this point a horrible sound gurgled from the stench of the sewer. It took on the shape of an enraged gargoyle[xi] spitting red and detritus. Peneth pulled me farther along the inner edge of the sewer path.

The gargoyle, standing to a full and ominous height and shaking its fist as we sailed by, spoke. "I rule here. Leave or I will suck you forever into the full power of this place. Mark my words: Do not try to cross this gutter. You will not leave."

Parked along the side of the trench were three amphibious vehicles, guns protruding[xii] and aimed into the flowing sewage below. Peneth ran ahead, then seemed to negotiate with the operator of one of the vehicles. She turned to me and motioned toward the most remote of the odd boat-plane contraptions[xiii].

"Hurry Adderley," Peneth beckoned. "We have only a few minutes to cross before the gargoyle can lay his hands on us."

We boarded and were carried, gargoyle howls behind us, to the island on the other side of the trench.

"This Sixth Circle island and the Seventh Circle beneath it are our final destinations. They will be our greatest challenges yet," Peneth warned me. "In the circles above you saw the punishments for those whose transgressions were mainly due to omissions and self-indulgences. Having said that, there is no excuse for them, for lack of awareness and self-indulgence by those we entrust with institutional power and resources are betrayals that affect all of us. So they deserve their eternal suffering.

"Those you will meet in the final two circles, though, are in this Inferno for *malicious* dereliction. They are in the last circles because by their deeds they continually and knowingly injured others and prevented the growth, full expression, and development of the people, groups, institutions, and countries they led. You saw the early manifestations of these sins when you met those suffering in the Circle of Ignorance and the Circle of Abdication. But in these last circles you will encounter willful and systemic damage to personal, institutional, and even global well-being."

We scrambled off the boat-plane, alighting onto a vast expanse of fiery-hot sand. The stench of the sewer we just crossed lingered, even as a dust spout twirled towards us. I was so stunned by the heat and furor of its approach that I didn't notice where I was stepping. I stubbed my toe on a sharp metal object and fell across what was an ankle-high, narrow metal box. Before the sand storm became too dense for me to see anything, I realized that the box was covered with precious but dirt-encrusted jewels. It was padlocked shut and sat in a slippery, shallow puddle of hot, red ooze. Steaming rivulets drained toward the sewer we just crossed.

Something stirred inside the box and I thought I heard someone talking, but only in a whisper. However, the whisper conveyed an indescribable agony. The box was too small to hold a body, yet I knew that it held some remnants of a person. The whisper accompanied a faint tapping from the inside. I put my ear to the keyhole.

From inside the box, but barely audible, I heard a voice. "Get me out of here," it said. "I am entombed in a place of absolute darkness, boiling. I can't see or move even though my voice and clatter bounce and amplify end-lessly against these rancid walls while I rot away. Get me out, get me out, get me out! I command this! You are my servant. Why are you not jumping at my requests? I am the boss, I have the power, do as I say . . . this minute do it! Can't you hear me pounding inside this cauldron? Don't you know who I am, you vulgar, scurrilous wretch? I make the rules, I do the thinking! How dare you treat me this way!"

I lifted myself back up, not wanting to take the abuse, and brushed the hot, wet, reddened sand from my pants. I did all this while trying to keep as much of my one bare foot off the steaming sand as possible. The sandstorm had passed and I widened my eyes from a squint to see that there were thousands of red-stained, sand-covered, jeweled boxes scattered throughout this part of the is-land. These people were buried alive in priceless tombs that were floating or sitting askew in slippery, steamy, shallow red puddles in this terrible desert.

I asked Peneth, "What are diamonds, emeralds, rubies and golden boxes doing in the Leadership Inferno? And what have those who are inside these treasure chests done to deserve being buried but aware of their entombment?"

She replied, "Why don't you ask one of them, Adderley, while I begin our preparations to enter the final circle of this terrible place."

I approached one of the smaller treasure boxes, for even though it was small, it had relatively more and bigger jewels. It simultaneously fascinated and horrified me, for

I had some idea about what it held. The red puddle was also bigger and flowed toward the sewer as if pumped from a never-empty artery. I bent down and repositioned the box so that I could kneel in a dry place. As I gingerly repositioned the box, the red stream flowed faster and there was a whisper of agony that penetrated my bones more than any imaginable scream.

From the box came words that I could only hear with my ear directly on the keyhole: "What infernal earthquake shakes this eternal prison? I am shattered, broken to fragments from the power of it."

I put my mouth to the keyhole and whispered, "I come from the living to learn the lessons of power here. Please tell."

The voice from the box answered, "Horrors. What hell-shattering sounds deafen me while rattling my every fiber? Stop. It reverberates, pure atom-smashing noise. STOP your screaming at me!"

I didn't know what was happening. My mere whisper and most delicate touches seemed to be amplified to super-human proportions for this entombed creature. I looked in fear and curiosity at the box.

"Oh what is the searing heat of invisible lasers that pierce me everywhere," said the voice in the box. "Stop, please stop them, withdraw them! You are a merciless jailor. Let me be, uninterrupted, in my endless pain and isolation."

Only then did I become aware of an army of guards, carrying a variety of weapons–guns, knives, swords–plus bullhorns and magnifying glasses. As they patrolled this desolate place, they kicked the jeweled boxes, yelled into bullhorns positioned at the keyholes, and held magnifying glasses to capture and focus the ever burning sun through the jewels and into the macabre little treasure chests.

I hesitated to approach the guards, but I had to know what was happening there. I mustered the courage to tentatively tap one on the shoulder.

The guard rattled, "What is it you want? You are an oddity here, for I can see that you still live. Oh, that I could have another chance."

"But you are a guard here, inflicting pain on these others," I answered. "Why do you do this and how has this become your fate?"

"During their lives, those who exist forever in these glittery tombs were entrusted with much power. They were formal leaders in a wide variety of institutions. They were responsible for the wise use of a massive array of resources–financial, human, capital, psychic. And they abused it. They used their power to dominate and subjugate, suppress and humiliate others, and advantage themselves while holding others back. They did not realize that as people with titles and institutional power, they were more than themselves: they occupied roles with powers and responsibilities bigger than themselves alone.

"These people, of both high and low rank, didn't realize that when they spoke as formal leaders, they actually roared as far as others were concerned. When they looked at something as leaders, their attention carried the energy of laser beams. When they walked down the hall or into someone's space, they shook the Earth. Then when they noticed that their words, attention, and movements carried these powers over others, they reveled in the subjugation, in the humiliation of others, in their ability to boss and control.

The guard pointed at a small box. "Over there, in that tiniest of boxes, rests one of the most power-abusing of national leaders. In that little one to your right," he said as he began pointing out other boxes, "is an executive of a big international corporation who reveled in taking people down, humiliating them in public places. Here, in front of us, is the everlasting tomb of a non-profit manager who used his position for personal aggrandizement, creating and intimidating a vast organization of 'yes-members.' He never truly amplified the tremendous creativity and influence of the people assembled for the cause. And this ornate box," he pointed to a round treasure chest to his left," "holds hundreds of those leaders who used their power and position to gain sexual and other advantages over others and to promote their cronies.

All of these power abusers now get what they doled out in life, not a bigger playground, but a smaller tomb; not the ability to shake and use and intimidate others, but the endless torture of being painfully shaken, burned, and sound-blasted.

With a particular relish he kicked the chest nearest us, "Here is a petty tyrant supervisor from a government agency you would recognize. Behind his desk he always posted a part of the organization chart, with his box bigger and on top. When I worked for him, he frequently pointed to his box saying, 'See this. This is ME, NOT YOU, so shape up.' That chart is buried with him, but his box on the chart is now the smallest and sits at the bottom of the flow. I like kicking his tomb, and when I feel especially mean, I scream into his keyhole describing all the priceless jewels that are forever both nearby and yet outside of his reach. I worked on his team and let him diminish and humiliate me. I colluded in my own diminishment, so my fate, not as terrible as his, is to forever be in a reverse role in this infernal desert."

I looked at the guard in horror at what I was hearing. My scabbed bare foot settled deeply into the hot sand and I couldn't move it. Something was making me fully face what was going on here. The burning seemed to be trying to expunge something from me and I realized that I had sometimes abused my rank. Did I do it on purpose? Did I enjoy putting people down? Was I aware of the impact of my judgments, my words, my presence? I cringed at my lack of awareness and I recalled my feelings when I was put down by my math teacher in high school, by my college engineering advisor. I also realized that as a "boss," I have felt some satisfaction from others' deference, enough to sometimes want deference for its own sake. My bare foot began to throb and bleed.

Peneth reappeared, reached into her tool bag and handed me an ointment, which I took and rubbed on top of my foot until it relaxed and I could lift it out of the sand. After a while, Peneth spoke to me. "YOU still have time, Adderley. Learn from what you see. Many here suffer multiple reverberations of their punishments because they abused their rank repeatedly and with relish. They also refused to do one of the most important things a great leader can do: encourage and require others to take on their own power and responsibility.

"The relationship between leaders and others, when it takes the form of domination and leader-worship, freezes people into dependency. This stunts ongoing growth and development and keeps organizations from being creative and adding the value that society needs and should expect. Our institutions fail all of us when there is this power abuse. With disproportionate power comes disproportionate responsibility for being aware, humble, and committed to the larger good, for service to something bigger than the self.

"I lecture you about this now because I see you are ready to hear what I have to say even though you have already started down a path in life that could lead you permanently to this horrible place. Remember what you see, for the lure of the jewels of rank and power will haunt you even more in your new, more far-reaching vice president role once you are back home."

As I listened to Peneth, I felt sick. My stomach rumbled. The sense of pending personal catastrophe, the horror of all this suffering almost knocked me out. I wanted to do anything to get away from there, especially since I knew the worst was ahead.

She wouldn't let me get relief. Instead we headed deeper into the desert.

We walked and walked, the sun ever bigger above and around. At some point, we were in a place where there were no more jeweled tombs or taunting guards . . . nothing but endless heat, sand, and sun. Peneth said nothing and it was clear I shouldn't speak. I fell into myself in an agonizing, wordless self-reflection, feeling that my inner world was an abyss.

After either an instant or an eternity, I looked down at my feet, crunching the sand alternately with the very different sounds of a shoe step and a bare footstep. Even as I limped, my feet moved in a rhythm, like a prayer or mantra. Peneth was beside me. My eyes were scratchy and my sight hazy from the whirling sand. Before I saw it with somewhat clearing eyes, I was aware of something new on the horizon.

It appeared first as a slight protuberance with a wisp of something above it. Closer, closer, a lonely mountain–bigger, bigger. Not just smoking, but belching hard things and flames. I blinked to clear my view, for it seemed that ghostly human forms rose in filmy ripples from the top. A Vesuvius lay ahead–eerie, menacing. No lava residue beneath it, although it clearly spewed something like lava, heavy and molten.

Peneth broke the silence. "Only a desert as vast as eternity can contain this horrific place that we are about to visit, Adderley. I see that since we entered the Inferno you have sweated out many of the parts of you that would have been burned in the crater we will now enter. From this point on you will not sweat, for your sweat would boil. However, your new awareness will make you far more sensitive to the angst and pain of the choices you will see than if you had remained unaware–or some would say, 'innocent.' Your most difficult lessons remain to be learned."

We were getting close enough to the volcano to feel its presence. It was more than heat, for heat has limits–a vanishing point, like absolute zero, where matter and energy turn into something else and new rules apply. Something other than what my human senses could detect was there. Aware of the absurdity of sensing something I couldn't sense, I had an uncanny trust in the process that I was finding or was finding me. Yet I felt I was also losing myself. Not yet dead, I sensed a sliver of a new option. A choice.

Then I heard a strange and alluring voice. "Adderley, stop this fruitless quest. Go back to your world of the living and continue as you were. You don't need all these lessons. Knowing what goes on here will just confuse you and keep you from living the good life. Go back. Peneth's way is too difficult and complicated." As it spoke I was faintly aware of a seductive cool and hazy light just beyond my reach.

I spoke to that strange voice, a slight coolness brushing through me. "I'm not sure that leadership is for me. Maybe I need to stop before I succumb to the temptations of the powers that I've been asked to take on. My faults so far are small. I don't think I am strong enough to take on other leadership roles."

Peneth noticed that I was in distress. She came to me and took my hand, leading me slowly forward. I walked for a while, then felt frozen in my tracks.

The strange and eerie voice filled my head for a second time. "Adderley, you are not able to continue. Stop now and cut your losses. What lies ahead is frightening beyond imagination. You are not strong. You have already fallen into many power seduction traps. Stop and tell Peneth to release you."

The bright cool light came closer. It was so soothing. I was tired of the pain, the heat, the terrible price I was paying for having formal power. I didn't want to face the ghouls that seduce and might continue to haunt me as a formal leader.

I took steps toward the cool light, which now contained sounds of early morning lapping water at the edge of a calm sea. Peneth shook me back to my current reality.

"Adderley, wake up. You are being tempted out of the very state that is your salvation. Come with me now and face the full powers of a universe that needs stewardship from the wise and the seasoned. You have endured and learned much and earned the right to the last lesson. Wake up!"

I shook my head, Peneth's encouragement pulling me out of a dreamy lull. I turned back in her direction.

The strange voice intervened for a third time. "This is your last chance, Adderley. Stop this ridiculous, hubristic quest now and avoid the torture that awaits you in the last Inferno circle. Everything you need, everything you could want in life awaits you, for you have power on earth that few have ever experienced. You have earned it. You have worked for it. Your amazing talents deserve the rewards that come with the thankless task of being a formal leader. Why deny yourself the benefits? Who says you have to sacrifice when you already sacrifice by giving yourself to this organization that cares about nothing other than profits anyway? You deserve a share in what you create and the people below you should be grateful that you are at the helm. Leave this horrible place now and I will be your guide to wealth and fame and fortune like you have never before seen. I see you are bleeding and all it takes is your agreement here, signed with your own blood, to be forever released from the stress of all this responsibility."

A shadowy figure presented me with a document, offered a pen, and drew blood into the pen from drops left by my naked and raw foot.

I was tempted, ready to sign, when flashes of all the Inferno Circles I had visited converged into one vision. I saw the people in the antechamber to this horrible place. They couldn't decide whether to accept the mantle of leadership or not, and continued to run in circles around the decision, dizzy. Then I saw the Ignorant of the First Circle. They accepted the formal leadership role but remain forever unaware of what that means. The First Circle was rapidly eclipsed by the Second Circle residents: the Myopics who, even though they had some power over the future, only complied with short-term pressures, unwittingly compromising what would happen in the long term.

My head was bursting but feeling very much alive as the residents of the Third Circle swirled past in my memory—half-brains looking for connection. These reductionists saw everything as either a problem to be managed rationally or an opportunity that could only live if free to float without tether or follow-through. The pain of those in the Third Circle was eclipsed as the Abdicators of the Fourth attempted to rise up and speak. Even though they knew what they should do, they left the most difficult leadership work to staff and held themselves above the systems and processes that they expected others to use. They are eternally punished by those they brought into their unholy and ineffective alliance.

Then, as I began to more deeply fathom the long-term and negative consequences of leadership abdication, Circle Five's Cowards swirled around me. These people who had the power and resources to act didn't speak up, didn't go counter to prevailing, seductive forces they believed to be dysfunctional or wrong. Although they often set out on a courageous direction, they lost muster and refused to steer the course during times of change and challenge. Because of them, major catastrophes occurred and great ideas that might have advanced the larger best interests lay aborted.

Even as I contemplated the lessons of the previous five circles of omission and self-indulgence, I was overwhelmed by The Sixth Circle's abusers of rank. I sat where I was and sobbed, with tears from depths I have never known, in mourning for the damages that abuses of power have done to individual and institutional psyches and perhaps even to our ability to survive on the planet.

I thought that maybe this was all too much for me. Maybe I should sign this pact with the devil and be done with it— enjoy the earthly fruits of power while I can. For at that moment I was not confident that I could rise above it all.

The way forward in this Inferno looked indescribably desolate. I fell into a total and a horrific depression. I was aware of the magnitude of life and all its promise. Yet I yearned for death and its reprieve, solace, comfort, escape from all pain and from the angst of "should's" and "could's." Feeling a deep pressure in my chest and finding it difficult to breathe, I craved the final terminal resting and relief.

I was clearly at a crossroads—a confusing place—and the point of total decision where I had to decide whether to live or die—the place where there was no option and perhaps all options. I knew that I had to act and that every act would have a consequence that I could see or surmise—now, tomorrow, the next day, and into infinity!

Then I felt a surge of something new inside of me. I was aware that Peneth was near, but she was not pulling or pushing me anywhere. She stood detached from it all, seeming to wait for me to decide.

I felt that I knew too much and yet not enough. I sensed a tug from some deeper purpose within me, something that I have been vaguely aware of since I was a child. I was standing at the crossroads but somehow better equipped to do what needed to be done.

Without any further thought, I stood up and started marching towards the volcano.

"I'm ready for this last lesson, Peneth. Whether I will survive it or not, I'm not sure. But I'm glad you're with me and I will do what I need to do so that I can return as a better leader or, maybe, decide to decline the offer."

"Let's be off," Peneth said.

The Lesson: Be a leader who is RESPECTFUL in your thoughts and interactions.

CHAPTER 14
Seventh Circle:
The Corrupt
and Corruptors

Apparently I was walking while dreaming, for the volcano that seemed so far off was now just ahead of us: vast, belching, ominous, alive. Four enormous obelisks poked from the ground around it, creating four equidistant corner towers appearing to guard the decapitated mountain. The dread I felt requires words that haven't yet been invented, for the feeling was beyond description.

Peneth stepped in front of me and gestured for me to slow my pace. As we got closer I saw that the towers were actually comprised of the torsos of hundreds of once-human forms.

Peneth spoke in hushed tones. "The ruler here has chosen his guardians well, Adderley. He has surrounded his most terrible circle with the collective but headless spirits of those who once had great formal power but used it in twisted ways to reverse the constructive evolutionary forces that lie at the heart of all nature. They were corrupt and their actions spread corruption like a deadly virus – almost destroying what the life-force behind evolution had built up."

A great and thunderous rumble erupted as the towers spewed what appeared to be insults and profanities in too many languages to count. I was mystified that the welded bodies that were the towers could speak, for I saw no heads. The "speech" was actually the result of tapping and scraping from somewhere within, a kind of auditory brail.

"These forms would return us to pre-Babel times," Peneth explained, "before human knowledge, communication, and the intermingling of races and cultures made us aware of both our individual gifts and our interdependencies. Those interred here built vast regimes through fear and divisiveness. They appealed to and amplified the shadow powers we all harbor–the dark sides of power, wealth, pleasure.

"To our right is Discor, the combined spirit of religious leaders who preached and incited hatred and violence under the guise of one true faith or by claiming elite and special access to supernatural powers.

"On the left is Excretious, a cacophony of national leaders, leaders of political and national movements, politicians and public officials of all kinds and at all levels who stole from the people–trust as well as money. They took bribes, robbed national coffers and sent the wealth into their own bank accounts, bent justice and systems to their own ends, and produced bureaucratic excrement rather than value-adding services. Some, through genocide, knowledge-control, and oppression stunted and destroyed the people, institutions, and nations they led.

"In front of us, speared and gored by multitudes of inventions and programs gone awry, is Rapious. Look closely and you will recognize business and union leaders who distorted their organizations to optimize their own prestige and financial gain, plundering and destroying their institutions while creating cancerous cultures that would replicate abuses and breeches. Many who are forever joined together there actually demolished their institutions. Their organizations exist no more except as derided memories and excuses that others point to in order to draw attention away from their own shameful and nefarious actions."

"You can't see the tower, Perjurous, for it is behind the volcano. The cement that joins the creatures there is particularly painful. In life they ran non-profit and educational institutions that had high motives–to feed the poor, to bring education and spiritual enlightenment to those without access, to spread peace in the world, to eradicate diseases, to help others during disasters, to provide legal and psychological advice and counsel others, to create a knowledgeable and humane next generation. But those who are doomed to this place took advantage of those whose good works and wealth they enlisted. These horrific souls diverted funds and resources to selfish ends and lied about it, fabricating information and covering up their tracks. Some simply trickled off resources, padding the administrative costs. Others committed fraud on grander scales–despicable breaches of trust.

"Collectively, these heinous actors worked to distort a natural order that values life, interdependency, trust, and evolution. Fortunately, they did not terminally damage our social fabric or our optimism, but it will be up to today's leaders–both formal and informal–to make sure that the more important constructive forces get stronger and more viral. But more on that later, Adderley. This Seventh Circle has yet to teach its lessons. To learn them we must descend into the Pit."

Peneth then led me on until we stood at the foot of Rapious. I shuddered at what I saw–a pillar of torsos glued together as one. Raspy, angry sounds of all kinds in languages I didn't know filled the air around me.

Suddenly, Peneth issued an order. "Rapious, this sojourner with me is from your clan, but he lives and has yet to complete his destiny. I command you to lift us up and set us down in the volcanic depths of the Seventh Circle so that he can learn the last truths about what brings you all here and damns you to eternal punishment!"

At this command, a ferocious blast of lava exploded from the volcano. The already red sky darkened to a foreboding maroon that was set against a dirty yellow and black haze. Rapious, the tower of torso fragments in front of us, bent slowly. A giant charred, shovel-like mitten creaked toward us, the creaks clearly profanities. In one clumsy swoop, we were scooped up and lifted high above the spewing lava, which like a spitting fountain had a hole in its center.

Terrible dissonant chords emitted from the depths of the volcano. They were beyond screams—the inverse of music—filling and haunting and rending the atmosphere. As we descended into the void, Peneth told me to cover my ears and find the center of myself, the center that called me to take and then continue this journey. I rested in that place until I felt us sliding off Rapious' mitted hand.

Once in the depths of the volcano, I sensed a different kind of burning. At that moment I thought about a Robert Frost poem I'd read years ago--something about ice being as powerful a way to end the world as fire.[xiv]

I shuddered, freezing cold—a burning cold—freezer burn. Above, the spewing lava continued its fierce roar. But here in the pit of hell was a vast frozen landscape, everything ice and frozen boulders. Eerie, the glow was reddish. I had never felt such searing, burning cold, but I was able to move and didn't feel in danger of being immobilized. My bare foot was, however, in excruciating pain with blisters on blisters. There were caves in the distance and holes in the ice floor that beckoned. I caught a glimpse of a very far away flailing movement.

Peneth reverted to explaining mode. "There are three sections of Circle Seven that I want to show you, Adderley. In all parts of this horrendous circle of the Inferno you will see the suffering of those who were corrupt and who corrupted others—those without empathy and devoid of ethical sense, whose net effect on earth was the deliberate destruction of institutions, of spirit, of people, of hope and optimism, of future generations. You will have read about some of these people who subverted their leadership positions. They left legacies of destruction and distrust that haunt those who would be ethical in their use of formal powers. Come."

We reached a small ice-cave and stooped to enter it. There were howls and discordant, high-pitched, would-be arias all seeming to compete for a non-existent stage. When I adjusted my eyes to the dim light, I saw an endless reach of little heads poking out from the ice below and the ice-walls beside and above. They were arranged in clusters of diverse colors, genders, and ages. Individuals in each group faced all others and could only move their heads in a radius that kept the others in view. They were very close to each other and clearly were filled with hatred for what they saw. Their tongues could lash out at each other, at which point, deep gashes accompanied by a dreadful stench appeared on and around the faces of the victimized. But all were victims of each other's hatred and shared the same fate.

I had to know what they had done to doom them to this strange and horrific destiny. "Who are you and why are you punished this way, forever frozen with people different than you and whom you obviously hate?" I asked.

One of the heads spoke up. "We all received the same dreadful sentence, although we forever and hopelessly fight for repeal. They say that our authoritarian ways and reigns of fear created rampant internal sickness in our institutions. They say that we hated diversity and favored only those who were like us and pandered to us, and that in this process we perpetuated generations of bigoted and tainted leadership under us and after us. Well, as horrific as this place is, we would all do it again in a nano-second. Why shouldn't we have had our astronomical rewards at the expense of the chattel? Or why would we not deserve the spoils of our decisions as the elected elite? We made the big decisions and even led revolutions. We deserved to make the institutions in our own likeness.

"Bah!" He spits at the head across from him. "See the fear in her eyes? It's the only pleasure I have in this despicable place." As he said this, the head on his right lashed out and inflicted a gash, stopping his speech, while a flicker of perverse pleasure registered in his tormentor's eyes.

Peneth described things further. "The unrepentant souls in this first part of Circle Seven created destructive cultures in the organizations they led. They pitted different groups against each other to maintain control. They hated diversity and created a 'be like me and support me or else' standard. They left a legacy of pandering, fear, win-lose behavior, and domination hierarchy in their wake.

In addition, what is terribly sad is how very easy it was for them to create these cultures and how extremely difficult it has been for the leaders who followed them to turn the situation around. Negative and cutthroat cultures are a lasting legacy, Adderley, meriting the perpetrators a place in this deepest circle of Leadership Inferno. The only consolation is that they will now forever live as underlings in the kind of cultures they created while alive."

I couldn't respond, for I was thinking about experiences I'd had or heard of. I'd seen a number of institutional and team cultures that were tainted this way or were in various stages of devolution. Even though I knew that many leaders don't follow this destructive model, I was pulled to wallow in the shadow side again, as if to snatch a life lesson from it. As I was about to formulate my thought, Peneth gently urged me on.

"Adderley, the next section of this Circle makes yet another point about the corruption that leaders are tempted to."

We ducked out of the first cave and slipped and slid—my foot in horrific pain—toward another, smaller cave. We had to worm our way in on our stomachs. The roof was so low we could only wiggle into a sitting position. In this little cave were uncountable numbers of rolling heads the size of golf balls, eyes bulging, neck skin jagged. Something unseen was striking them, creating a riot of bouncing balls moving in all directions and frequently bouncing off each other.

"Through their actions and decisions," Peneth said, "the people interred here created false rosy pictures for their institutions and themselves as formal leaders while at the same time doing grave and often irreparable damage beyond their organizations. Some deliberately allowed toxic waste to spew into the environment or denuded endangered natural resources without replenishing. Some of them subjected their workers to unsafe and unhealthy work conditions. They did this knowing that injury, illness, and even death could result. Some spent vast sums of money and other capital that they didn't have, passing enormous debts on to future generations.

"Others knowingly created and propagated products that were unsafe and ultimately harmful in other ways. They hid the results of their own research when those results would damage their reputation or ability to succeed. Some preached fear and created dissention and hatred toward other groups, creating rivalries and conflicts that decimated beautiful lands and peoples and energized cycles of ongoing hatred, genocide, and retribution. *Everyone here passed major negative consequences into the future for others to address...and they did this KNOWINGLY!*"

I was overcome with disgust. "Whew. Let's leave this place. The lessons are excruciating and I am beginning to feel my own head being knocked around by awesome forces."

We slithered out of the second cave. There were other caves just like it in the distance, but Peneth walked away from them to what appeared to be a large, open span of ice. As we crossed it, the flailing object that I noticed before grew bigger, and I realized that it was a scorpion-like creature with three heads, stuck in the ice.

"What you see ahead of us is the Devil itself," Peneth explained. "Dante described it well in his Inferno – for the devil's three heads show it for what it is: ignorant, impotent, and filled with hatred. He is forever stuck in this infernal ice, filled with hatred and an anger that reaches to the ends of the universe. He knows he will never be able to destroy the natural order of things, even though he remains, for now, part of the spirit that tempts us all to take the infernal path.

"We won't directly confront him, Adderley, but we need to see a bit more of the consequences of the unholy alliances he has forged with those once living and who reside here."

At this point, I saw a series of holes in the ice. One was nearby. It was actually a tunnel. Peneth warned me that we were entering the third section of this Circle of Corruption. We took icy steps down into one of the holes. The cold burned more fiercely than ever and I felt a terminal deadly assault on my heart, lungs, and brain from the pressure and pain of the freeze. A frosty wind blurred everything with a frozen mist that was permeable enough for us to walk through. I could barely think and my eyelids were slow to move. I feared being frozen forever within this hole.

Then, with a new clarity, I noticed what was happening here. Very tiny gumball-size heads were imbedded totally under the ice. I saw severe strain and stress on their faces, but their surroundings kept them prisoners, and the continuous frozen mist seemed to add incessant layers of burning cold to their prison. As I tried to figure out what this punishment was all about, I bumped into a machine that seemed to be maintaining the tunnel and the continuous laying of ice. The operator was a mini version of the three-headed Satan figure that ruled this place. He turned one of his heads to face me and I was confronted with a Cyclops head. I drew on all the inner strength that I had mustered in preparing to take this last part of the journey and felt a wellspring of protection surge from within. I tried to move past him so I could find a way to communicate with those buried there.

"Don't even try to talk to these...my most dear blood brothers and sisters." Cyclops growled. "They sold their souls to us long ago. Playing God in life, they made their own rules and laws. Some sanctioned industrial spying. Others, including from the media, created incentives that encouraged continual muck-raking, character assassination, and the continual destruction of hope and optimism. Still others that you see here created intrigues and swindles—like complex financial packages or Ponzi schemes—or they accepted bribes. In all cases they willfully interfered with the constructive sequences of cause and effect and confused the natural order of things so that they could manipulate results to their own selfish ends. Their punishment is to be totally out of control in a very small world where they have no power at all—and where the cause-effect consequences are very clear and very painful. A few..."

At this point, I put up a hand to stop his tirade, but he continued. "A few who lie in indescribable agony here built institutions and fostered laws and policies that placed some groups beneath others, effectively enslaving them. Others invented and sustained '-isms' and conceptual frameworks, like the Cold War, or intercultural 'jihad' that ensured broad and sustained mayhem and actions based on unquestioned assumptions. Some directed dissention and hatred at competitors, rival political groups, races, social and cultural groups, and even nations. The antagonisms that some of those here sowed from their power positions extended broadly and for many generations and are even at work on Earth today."

I turned to Peneth, "So, those buried here did heinous things that created many negative ripple effects, beyond direct and immediate consequences. I can see why they are in a place where they can neither move nor cause anything to happen!"

The Cyclops head that had been talking sneered and joined his other two heads to resume construction and maintenance work. Peneth and I squeezed past him and walked without speaking, past the innumerable residues of the once powerful who were buried here. For eternity they would continue to be small and powerless, while in pain and aware.

I have no idea how far or how long we walked. But eventually the tunnel widened. There seemed to be an opening ahead. But there was increasing darkness accompanied by what I can only describe as a soul-rattling, surreal dirge. I was sure that this dreadful requiem used octaves well below what the human ear can hear—from hell's own phantom organ. Yet, I was aware of the "music." Again I realized that being in this place had somehow endowed me with the extra senses needed to experience it.

As we walked with a sense of destiny, I wondered about power. Is it a gift or a curse? Many of those I had just passed could have taken a different course. If they had, what would have been the result? Are those on whom we bestow authority really able to prevent the catastrophes they seem to drive or help create? If those incarcerated here had made more ethical choices would there have been no genocide? No racism? No passing of problems on to new generations? Would their followers (clearly they are also culpable!) have been better partners for better institutions, nations, the world? Would all of us be richer? Safer? Healthier? Better stewards of the planet and its resources? Would we be more accountable, responsible, free, fulfilled?

Is it possible for there to be a universe without evil? Most religious scriptures and native creation stories tell of early times when there was perfect harmony, innocence, and acknowledged interdependence of all things. But they also tell of the eventual intrusion of evil, of the dark side, of temptation, of a fall, of entering a time of choice and personal responsibility. The implication in most spiritual and philosophical traditions is that, for there to be choice, there must be opportunities to go either with or against the life force. Many of the great hero and heroine myths and tales draw energy from confrontations between "good" and "evil"; they dramatize the interplay of dark and light.

Some would say that without the shadow, we cannot know the light, and vice versa. Some would say that innocence causes its own destruction, just as today we are told to be vigilant as we walk in dangerous areas, for attackers will prey first on those who are not wary. And some would say that we all carry within us the seeds of both good and evil and that recognizing this creates the empathy that keeps us humble and alert.

Thinking about these things, I felt seduced into a dreamy space. My head was full of these thoughts, as though something was trying to come together for me that was vital for my future. Then a massive crashing and whipping sound brought me back to the frigid, burning tunnel.

Peneth and I had reached the edge of the ice-tunnel and faced a strange vibrating pillar covered by matted tufts of hair. Whirring, crackling sounds intermingled with the low-pitched dirge. I had the sense of being in the deepest sub-strata of the Earth—the place where everything boils, surrounded by death rattles, and where what rains as fire above is merely a cooling force.

Peneth now exuded urgency. "Adderley, climb quickly down by hanging onto and stepping in these matted and mottled tufts. Don't be distracted by the dirges you hear.

They will make you desire to jump off into the deepest pit below, for this is the place where the Devil will take your entire soul and try to convince you to come completely over to the dark side. Follow me, drawing on all the willpower you have developed on this journey."

We climbed down, ever in danger of being shaken off this foul-smelling tower of flesh and hair. We reached a strange web-shaped ledge that I realized was a monstrous foot.

It was the Devil's foot! It was stuck in a vice-like crevasse. I had been climbing down the devil's leg! The funeral dirge got louder and I almost succumbed to its allure.

Through a crack in the crevasse I saw the light of a morning sunrise and felt the breeze of an after-rain Spring day.

Peneth called to me, "Adderley, you must hurry. Jump off quickly and come through this crack in the rock."

I did as she said and arrived in the most beautiful place I had ever experienced. I felt light as air and on top of the world at sunrise. Above me were both the morning moon and the rising sun. Wispy clouds wended past, showering me with a gentle mist. I realized I was on a mountain, but felt suddenly disoriented since my journey had, so I thought, been progressively down. I was both invigorated and exhausted. I lay down in the wet grass and filled my chest with a luxurious, effortless, and deep breath of the fresh morning air.

The Lesson: Be A STEWARD of the resources and evolving potential in your care.

The Return

CHAPTER 15
Accepting the Calling

When I woke up, I was alone on top of what I realized was a small mountain. Flowers, butterflies, and colorful chirping birds were all around me. I saw a path and started down the hill. Above me a crow circled. When the path bifurcated, the bird flew ahead of me in the direction of one of the paths. I followed, trusting. The walk was refreshing. I still had only one shoe, but my foot's blisters had turned to calluses and there was only buffering, no pain.

After some distance I heard a rustle in the brush. A huge lizard–I think the one from my original dream–circled around me, showing its changing colors as it moved from tree trunk to flowers, to grass, to path. I felt no menace.

Then I saw a gate in the distance. It looked familiar. I headed towards it. But my path was obstructed; three little bear cubs were playing in front of me. I felt some fear, turned around and saw the mother bear lying off the path just behind me. She watched her cubs, watched me. Her gaze locked into mine, bringing all of my Inferno experiences back to me in one kaleidoscopic image that took but a fraction of a moment but made me think I had experienced a long and deep hibernation.

As I unlocked from this powerful exchange, I looked behind where she lay. The mountain I had just descended was the mountain from my original dream, one I could not then climb. I seemed to have come full circle but to be in a very different relationship with what was around me.

Then, I saw that there were actually two gates ahead. At this point the crow dropped an envelope onto the ground in front of me. I opened it.

Adderley, you have journeyed into the shadow side of power. You have been warned about the temptations that accompany formal leadership. You have seen seven grievous ways that those with formal power and authority fail in or subvert their roles:

Ignorance
Myopia
Reductionism
Abdication
Cowardice
Abuse
Corruption

The temptation to these will always be there if you accept a position of formal authority – one that puts disproportionate power into your hands.

But there are many rewards for accepting a leadership position and executing it wisely. These you have begun to discover.

I think you now realize that a leadership role offers three major opportunities that will significantly enhance your life and experience. First, as a formal leader you will have leverage. Through your decisions and actions you will help people and your institutions create more together than they could alone.

Second, your leadership role will challenge you to continuous learning and personal growth, for you will face many situations requiring increasing levels of consciousness, skill, and stretch.

And third, through your leadership role you will have the chance to leave a legacy: a legacy of a value-adding institution, a legacy of people who have developed through their association with you and the organizations you lead, and a legacy of greater social confidence that our institutions can work and be life-sustaining.

All this will be possible if in your work as a leader you are . . .

AWARE
BIFOCAL
SYNERGISTIC
ACCOUNTABLE
COURAGEOUS
RESPECTFUL
A STEWARD

You do have a choice. The gate at the left is one you should take if you find that formal leadership is not your calling in life. You may be drawn to another vocation. If so, the best choice for you is to walk through that door.

The gate on the right is for you if, knowing the shadow side, you are willing to take on the power, responsibilities, and challenges of a leadership calling. Open it only if it is the right one for you – and for what you now know to be the right reasons.

You decide. But decide with awareness of the responsibilities, opportunities, and temptations.

Peneth

I knew that I had made my decision, and I realized that I made it now for other reasons than those that led me to initially accept the vice president role at Jada. I made it because I knew that I have the abilities and the desire to lead. I felt more conscious about what this meant and more equipped to move forward with this decision. I thought I would be more alive by accepting the challenge than by running away from what I realized so clearly is my calling. I knew that I would continue to meet the shadows and be tempted by them, but I instinctively trusted that even though I would probably fail on many occasions, I could rise above the challenges I would face. I realized that I would become a better person because of this choice.

I turned the knob on the right side gate. The hinges creaked and screeched. I pushed the gate open, turned around and closed it carefully as though it was made of porcelain. I glanced at the little sign, "LI Retreat Center" but it faded away as I woke to the smell of roses and lilacs and slowly shook my head to see some of my best friends coming into focus.

"He's back with us," a voice said.

I slowly scanned the room, eyes landing on the edge of a note in my hand–barely visible under the covers.

It was a beautiful day, a few clouds that would be storms decorated the horizon outside my window, and there were double rainbows so near that I could almost touch them. The Jada campus lay just beyond my view.

AFTERWORD: LEADERSHIP AS A MYTHIC JOURNEY

In all mythic journeys including fairy tales, characters find themselves in places where they are lost, confused, challenged; where they must show their mettle. In forests, storms, deserts, tall towers, and prisons. On the high seas, in pursuit of impossible goals, the Odyssei, Rapunzels, Abrahams, Moseses, Luke Skywalkers, Beowulfs, Scrooges, Harry Potters, Christines, Red Riding Hoods–all confront inner and outer demons. They face challenges to their beliefs, virtues, and commitments. Even though it is not obvious or easy, they must select good or evil, the high or low road, and the path of virtue and creation or selfishness and destruction. They are potential heroes and heroines, stripped of excuses and steeped in the stark reality of their freedom to choose.

There can be no doubt that the call to leadership–to a position of formal authority–is a call to such a mythic journey. People in formal leadership roles operate on a larger-than-life stage—in a murky and fantastical context where "power tends to corrupt, and absolute power corrupts absolutely."[xv] The mysterious dark forests and stormy seas surrounding leaders are also haunted places. They are filled with ghosts—disembodied residue from the leader's own and others' past authority relationships with fathers, mothers, teachers, preachers, bigger or smarter kids, bullies. The institutional leader is thus both person and role, reality and fantasy.

For a leader it does no good to say, "But I am just me." Institutional leadership is, in part, a social construct, a reflection of what power means to a culture, to individual people, and at a point in time. But this doesn't take the leader off the hook. Rather it means that those who embark on the leader/manager journey have bigger shoes to fill even as they pursue their personal journey, for with greater power comes greater responsibility.

Formal leaders/managers (I use these terms interchangeably) must approach their task as a journey of mythic proportions at both the personal and societal levels. When this does *not* happen, at worst, dire consequences can occur. At best, the opportunity to leverage and create, as only institutions and individuals who are conscious of their power can, is lost—perhaps forever. These leaders become candidates, literally or figuratively, for the Leadership Inferno.

The question is, will the journey into the Leadership Inferno refine or co-opt? One way or another, the leadership role confronts formal leaders with this question.

What will be your choice?

POSTSCRIPT: A BRIEF SUMMARY OF DANTE'S "INFERNO"

The *Inferno,* the first of three sections in poet Dante Alighieri's *Divine Comedy,* is the inspiration for the approach I take in this book. Of course, it is brash to loosely pattern a book about formal leadership on one of the great moral poems of all time. Also, my focus on the *Inferno* without directly including parallels to Dante's other two *Divine Comedy* sections (*Purgatorio* and *Paradiso*) does risk leaving the reader in a hopeless frame of mind.

However, it's important to note that Dante, the main figure in his own comedy (traditionally meaning a story with a happy ending), does come out wiser and more fully aware and developed as a result of the Inferno part of his journey. The trip through the Inferno is crucial to Dante's ability to appreciate Paradise. In my story, our hero Adderley also grows and matures by facing the shadow side of leadership. He comes out of his experiences with a more textured appreciation of the important virtues that are inherently possible in the leadership role. Like Dante, he emerges with a knowledge of evil as well as good—a knowledge that will help him be more self-aware, self-managing, and a wiser leader.

Dante Alighieri lived in late thirteenth and early fourteenth century Italy (1265-1321). It was a time of high political intrigue saturated with power struggles between church and state and among families and groups representing the old feudal aristocracy and the emerging merchant class. These were the early days of what we would later label the Renaissance—the beginning of a major transformative time in the history of Western civilization.

Dante was a participant in and a victim of the tectonic social and political shifts around him. He was initially on top as part of the ruling class, but was later driven from his own Florence to die in exile. His entire poem is, in part, a retribution for his treatment: he places some of his enemies in various parts of hell and people he admires in purgatory and heaven. But he takes these personal liberties in the context of one of the great morality works of all time, drawing on religious, philosophical, and literary texts and insights, while creating an epic human development story.

The Story

Dante enters his Inferno through a dark wood—the archetypal symbol of the state of loss, confusion, self-doubt, and questioning that occurs during times of major transition and that (hopefully) precedes a new direction and rebirth. He admits his situation in the first sentence of his story:

> *"In the middle of the journey of our life, I came to myself in a dark wood where the straight way was lost."[xvi]*

Then he immediately steps out of the tale and consoles us that the ultimate outcome of his journey into the Inferno will be positive:

"So bitter is it, that scarcely more is death; but to treat of the good that I there found, I will relate the other things that I discerned."[xvii]

From his place in the woods he sees a distant mountain bathed in sunshine, but can't make his way to it. He is blocked by three animals: a leopard, a lion, and a wolf. He turns and runs away from the mountain, meeting the Roman poet Virgil (author of the epic poem, the *Aeniad*). Virgil will be his guide through the Inferno and Purgatorio. Virgil tells Dante that he has been sent by a higher spirit who is watching over Dante and wants him to take a journey. Virgil tells Dante that he cannot directly ascend the mountain, but must go through hell first. Virgil says,

"Wherefore I think and discern this for thy best, that though follow me; and I will be thy guide, and lead thee hence through an eternal place...."

So begins Dante's trek into the shadows. He enters through the Gates of Hell ("leave all hope, ye that enter"[xvii]), crosses a dark plain and the great river that surrounds hell, and enters limbo–the place of the unbaptized and the First Circle of hell. This circle is more a place of no hope than overt punishment.

From there they descend through the progressively more torturous levels of Circles Two through Five where people who lacked self-control and committed sins of passion reside. Guided by Virgil, Dante visits the Second

Circle of hell, seeing people who in life "subject(ed) reason to lust"[xix] buffeted by gale force winds. Then they trudge through the Third Circle, where people wallow in mud and rain "for the baneful crime of gluttony;"[xx] In the Fourth Circle they meet people who lacked moderation in use of wealth. These hoarders and spenders suffer constant conflict and unrest for their "ill-giving and ill-keeping."[xxi] Descending to the Fifth Circle they hear the pleas of the wrathful and slothful–the "souls of those who anger overcame"[xxii] and those who carried "lazy smoke within (their) hearts,"[xxiii] These perpetually accost each other or are entrapped in "black mire."

Circle Six brings Dante and Virgil to the devil's own city, Dis. Up to now, the sins punished in the Inferno have occurred because of human weakness, passion, lack of self-control, and disregard of reason and higher thinking. Beyond this point, however, people suffer for more egregious sins, for willful actions designed to destroy others in order to optimize themselves. Dante needs extra help to enter this part of the Inferno as a living person. He is accosted by several mythical evil forces: "...three Hellish Furies, stained with blood..." and Medusa, who if seen will "change him into stone."[xxiv] At this point, Virgil's help and rationality are not enough to get him through. An angel appears and the travelers pass through:

> *"Ah, how full he seemed to me of indignation! He reached the gate and with a wand opened it: for there was no resistance."*[xxv]

Dante's Sixth Circle is the place for heretics. Buried on a plain in iron tombs surrounded by flames, these are people who created their own sects and lured others to revere and follow them. Clearly these are transgressions of a different kind. For Dante, these and others in the lower Inferno levels have sinned in ways that reverse the divine in us:

> *"In this part are entombed with Epicurus all his followers, who make the soul die with the body."*[xxvi]

Dante's Seventh, Eighth and Ninth Circles are for those who damage and corrupt others, "whose end is injury;" who "either by force or by fraud, aggrieveth others."[xxvii]

In the Seventh Circle are three rungs, one each for those who do violence to others, themselves, or to nature. In the first rung, assassins, tyrants and murderers suffer in a river of blood. In the second, those who did violence to themselves have been turned into trees that produce poison.

> *"My soul, in its disdainful mood, thinking to escape disdain by death, made me, though just, unjust against myself."*[xxviii]

Then, in this part of the Seventh Circle, the stunted forest gives way to a hot desert, raining fire. Here those who desecrated nature and led others to pursue luxury rather than the good of the community either lie, sit crouched, or march incessantly. Virgil takes this opportunity to tell Dante about the source of all the streams of blood that they have seen. They originate in the tears of an old man whose head is gold, body is silver and bronze, and feet are clay–symbolizing a reverse evolution of humanity. The old man stands in Mount Ida, "which once was glad with waters and with foliage; now it is deserted like an antiquated thing."[xxix] Humans have turned Nature against herself and are being punished for it.

Dante's Eighth Circle has nine rungs. Everyone interred there has committed a deception–seducing, pandering, flattering, counterfeiting, being hypocritical, giving false counsel, forging, lying, using religious and political positions for personal gain. They suffer in hot filth and constraining holes, are pursued by birds and animals, prodded by demons, and trampled by others in the Circle. The suffering is greater for those who have had greater power and fame, including Ulysses, one of the great Greek leaders of the Trojan War, who because of his deceptions during life is only a voice in an eternal fire.

Near the end of this Circle, Dante loses his breath and sits down, exhausted. At that point Virgil reminds him about life's calling:

> *"Now it behooves thee thus to free thyself from sloth, … for sitting on down, or under coverlet, men come not into fame; without which whoso consumes his life, leaves such vestige of himself on earth, as smoke in air or foam in water; and therefore rise! Conquer thy panting with the*

soul that conquers every battle, if with its heavy body it sinks not down. A longer ladder must be climbed; to have quitted these is not enough; if thou understandest me, now act so that it may profit thee.[xxx]

The Ninth and last circle of Dante's Inferno is the place for those who broke special bonds of trust and love–who were traitors to relatives, country, friends, guests, and ultimately those in power under/over or service relationships. These are frozen in ice, possessed by demons, subjected to cannibalism, unable to express any thoughts or emotion. Giants who are frozen in place guard the center of this Circle – the place where Satan himself is entombed. He is covered with hair, has three heads, and bat-like wings whose flappings keep this part of hell frozen. Satan personally torments the worst traitors– represented by Judas and Brutus from religious and political history.

In a last symbolic act, Dante and Virgil climb down the hairy Devil, using the darkest creature as their final path into a dungeon gateway where their direction downward is suddenly reversed and they leave the Inferno and its lessons to begin their exploration of Purgatory and Paradise:

"We mounted up, he first and I second, so far that I distinguished through a round opening the beauteous things which Heaven bears; and thence we issued out, again to see the Stars."[xxxi]

For a free *Reader's Guide* and other support to help you implement the lessons and insights in this book, go to:

www.shadowsideofpower.com

FOOTNOTES

[i] See Postscript for a brief summary of the nine circles in Dante's Inferno

[ii] Bear is a symbol of hibernation, introspection

[iii] Lizard often stands for detachment from the ego, the power to regenerate and face fear, and to move in the underworld

[iv] Crow is both a symbol of ethical behavior, and fearless guidance in the dark.

[vv] The original sign in Dante's *Inferno,* warns, "Abandon every hope, all you who enter." (Canto II, Verse 9)

[vi] In Dante, the boatman, Charon, ferries the damned across the River Acheron and into the Inferno.

[vii] Minos, in mythology, was king of Crete and son of the Greek god Zeus and a human noblewoman, Europa. He is the judge of the dead in the mythical underworld. In Dante's *Inferno,* Minos has a long tail that wraps around the damned, hurling them to the circle of hell that is appropriate for their earthly transgressions.

[viii] Furies: Greek deities associated with vengeance and punishment.

[ix] Medusa: Raped by the sea god, Poseidon, by some accounts was originally a beautiful priestess in Athena's, the goddess of wisdom, temple. Athena turned Medusa

into a monstrous form with serpents for hair in order to protect her from further assaults. Her look was so fearsome that anyone seeing her turned into stone. In the Leadership Inferno her brief appearance also reminds us of the rage of the feminine at the long dominance of authoritarianism (traditionally viewed as a masculine energy).

[x] In Dante's *Inferno,* as Dante and his guide, Virgil, moved into the lower depths of hell, it took additional divine intervention by an angel to overcome the dark forces that would block their progress.

[xi] The sewer, the analogue of the River Styx in Dante's *Inferno,* is the second of three symbolic crossings. In the Leadership Inferno, the sewer separates upper from lower hell.

[xii] In Dante, Centaur—half man, half horse creatures— patrol the blood river, shooting arrows at anyone who tries to escape

[xiii] In Dante's *Inferno* this role is played by the centaur, Nessus, who is ordered by Chiron, the lead Centaur, to carry Dante and Virgil across a moat.

[xiv] See Robert Frost, "Fire and Ice," in The Poetry of Robert Frost, E.C. Latham, ed. Atlanta: Henry Holt and Company. 1923, 1969.

[xv] John Emerich Edward Dalberg Acton, first Baron Acton (1834–1902).

[xvi] Dante Alighieri, *The Divine Comedy*, The Carlyle-Okey-Wicksteed Translation (New York: Vintage Books, 1950), 11.

[xvii] Dante, *The Divine Comedy*, 14.

[xviii] Dante, *The Divine Comedy*, 22.

[xix] Dante, *The Divine Comedy*, 32.

[xx]   Dante, *The Divine Comedy*, 37.

[xxi] Dante, *The Divine Comedy*, 41.

[xxii] Dante, *The Divine Comedy*, 43.

[xxiii] Dante, *The Divine Comedy*, 43.

[xxiv] Dante, *The Divine Comedy*, 50.

[xxv] Dante, *The Divine Comedy*, 53.

[xxvi] Dante, *The Divine Comedy*, 54.

[xxvii] Dante, *The Divine Comedy*, 60.

[xxviii] Dante, *The Divine Comedy*, 73.

[xxix] Dante, *The Divine Comedy*, 78.

[xxx] Dante, *The Divine Comedy*, 129.

[xxxi] Dante, *The Divine Comedy*, 184.

ACKNOWLEDGEMENTS

This has been a work in progress and a personal development experience for over five years. During that time, many people read various drafts and offered comments that have made this a more powerful book. I am grateful to everyone who helped along the way, many of whom have graciously provided testimonials and reviews of this book.

Special thanks to my friends in the Woodlands Group, a think tank that continues to explore and promote ideas and actions that will make the world and our institutions better. And to my dear friend, Kevin O'Sullivan, who diligently helped me through several edits.

In addition, gratitude goes to professional colleagues in the leadership and human development communities. Every day they work to inspire and develop the kind of leadership we desperately need in these complex, exciting, and sometimes dangerously interconnected times.

I have had advice from psychologists and organization development specialists whose professional work focuses on how our institutions and we change and develop. I am very grateful for your support and teaching.

Thank you, too, to the many leaders in both the private and public sectors with whom I have been privileged to work during my four decades advising organizations on management and change issues. These leaders live with the awesome burden of formal power every day. They have been my clients, but also my teachers. I am grateful for the trust they place in me as they struggle to make decisions where the best option is seldom clear, and where there are often very difficult tradeoffs and contradictions. Lessons from their lives and challenges helped shape the selection of leadership virtues and vices that that appear in *The Shadow Side of Leadership*.

For this important gift and for everyone's help, I say, "Thank you!"

I also want to acknowledge the formative process of the book itself. Writing it has made me more conscious of my own leadership practices, potential, impact, and shortcomings. Books are amazing teachers to their authors, for every book begins as an idea that begs to be born, an ache or yearning to make sense of things, a spirit that yearns for embodiment. A book also provides a special way to reach out to the world and to engage it in important conversations—whether the author is physically present or not.

With this thought in mind, I would love to hear from you. pat@patmclagan.com.

ABOUT THE AUTHOR

Pat McLagan is an award-winning management consultant, entrepreneur, author, and speaker. A *Fortune Magazine* top 20 global executive called her work "seminal...leading to coherence, of culture and purpose... liberating."

She has helped implement major change, leadership, and strategy management initiatives in organizations as diverse as the General Electric Company, 3M, NASA, SABMiller, The US Defense Intelligence Agency, AT&T, Citibank, and the State of Georgia (USA).

She is the 15th person and second woman inducted into the Human Resource Development (HRD) Hall of Fame, is an elected member of the International Adult and Continuing Education Hall of Fame, and one of 100 "Inspiring Minds for a Century" from the University of Minnesota College of Education and Human Development. She has received many leadership awards, including the American Society for Training and Development's highest award for professional and community contribution and the 2012 Thought Leader Award by the Instructional Systems Association.

She holds degrees in English literature (BA, Phi Beta Kappa) and adult education (MA) from the University of Minnesota, is an honorary Professor of Human Resource Management, and has served on many professional journal advisory boards. She is featured as one of Tom Peters "Cool Friends."

Her papers and articles have appeared in *T+D Magazine*, *MWorld* and *The President* (American Management Association), the *Journal for Quality and Participation*, *Government Executive Magazine*, *The Conference Board, World Business Academy Perspectives*, and in other publications and handbooks.

Ms. McLagan has served on the governing boards of the American Society for Training and Development, the Instructional Systems Association, and the Minneapolis United Way, and is past chair of the board of directors for the Desmond Tutu Peace Foundation. She has three grown sons, three grandchildren, and while living in the United States, maintains personal and professional relationships in South Africa, where she lived in the 1990s.

Connect with Pat McLagan

Email: pat@patmclagan.com
Book site: www.shadowsideofpower.com
Blog: www.patmclagan.com/blog
Website: www.patmclagan.com

Twitter: http://twitter.com/patmclagan
Linkedin: http://www.linkedin.com/in/patmclagan

Free **Readers Guide** and access to other resources at
www.shadowsideofpower.com

OTHER BOOKS BY PATRICIA (PAT) MCLAGAN

Change Is Everybody's Business

The Age of Participation: New Governance for the Workplace and the World (co-authored with Christo Nel)

On-the-Level: Performance Communication That Works (co-authored with Peter Krembs)

Made in the USA
San Bernardino, CA
23 October 2014